WEIRD CULTURE KIDS

WEIRD CULTURE KIDS

NGỌC (BI) NGUYỄN

NEW DEGREE PRESS

WEIRD CULTURE KIDS

ISBN   978-1-63676-611-9 *Paperback*

         978-1-63676-279-1 *Kindle Ebook*

         978-1-63676-278-4 *Ebook*

CONTENTS

"You get a strange feeling when you're about to leave a place, I told him, like you'll not only miss the people you love but you'll miss the person you are now at this time and this place because you'll never be this way ever again."

AZAR NAFISI, *READING LOLITA IN TEHRAN: A MEMOIR IN BOOKS*

INTRODUCTION

———

I was very young when I realized my upbringing was different from that of the majority of the kids in Vietnam. Growing up in a wealthier-than-average Vietnamese family, I was given a very privileged and international upbringing—one that was not at all common in Vietnam in the early 1990s.

Unlike me, my parents were Cold War kids who took pride in their Soviet heritage, an important element of their identity since many years of their youth were spent in Moscow for their higher education and professional careers. They, too, were very privileged in their own time and context, since they managed to escape the war in Vietnam while getting the best education that was offered to them in the USSR, Vietnam's then strongest ally. But because they didn't grow up in a globalized world or learn how to properly adapt to it, both of them suddenly became very ill equipped to raise "weird culture kids" like my big brother, Phan, and myself.

In fact, culturally speaking, Phan and I were extremely weird. We were both born in Moscow and raised by parents who were Vietnamese but believed themselves to be somewhat Soviet—a nationality that no longer existed by the time we both started to understand the notion of nation-states and the inherited identity that was shared among the same people. To make matters worse, under the pressure of our French-educated grandparents, we were both enrolled in the French international school when I was three and Phan was five.

Mom and Dad could never help us with our homework because they didn't speak a word of French. Instead, they spent their days and nights making sure my brother and I were also fluent in both spoken and written Vietnamese because, according to them, the contrary would be like a second wave of French colonization. Naturally, my parents carried their allegiance to the Eastern Bloc proudly and, as a consequence, they couldn't communicate with our friends and their parents, who automatically belonged to the Western one.

This was the daily context in which I grew up: Vietnamese with a splash of Soviet culture at home coupled with a very French rearing at school. I was always in the middle, not entirely Vietnamese but also not fully French. Although it was sometimes confusing and conflicting to grow up among these different cultures, it was simply the norm for a small bunch of us.

I guess it was time to burst that bubble.

I left Vietnam at the age of fifteen to attend an American boarding school in Connecticut, and ever since then one of the most recurring questions people have asked me whenever we first met was *"Where are you from?"* This had always been one of the hardest questions for me to answer because I had never believed we should—could?—be "from" one place. I was never sure what type of information the speaker was trying to get from my answer. Was he trying to figure out where I was living before arriving here? Or did she want to know where I was born? Or, going beyond the geographical dimension, which cultures shaped my personality and which sets of beliefs dictated my behavior?

Dodging this question was never an option due to the nation-state paradigm that we currently lived in. It was very normal and acceptable for people to ask strangers and newcomers this question, socially speaking. With time and experience, I learned the answer to this four-word question was supposed to not only give me a strong sense of identity, but also give those around me a strong sense of who they were dealing with.

Despite this common practice, nothing accurate had ever come out of this question.

Naturally, my go-to answer had always been Vietnam because that was the country of my passport, and my whole family still lived there. But personally, I have never fully felt Vietnamese. I was born in Moscow, grew up in Hanoi, and enrolled in the French school at the age of three upon my return to the "homeland." I knew how to write in French before I learned to do so in my mother tongue. Most other Vietnamese kids told me I was very *Tây*—a Vietnamese expression that literally translated to "the West" in English.

My parents brought me up in a nostalgic world they created at home where they often spoke about their time in the USSR, listened over and over again to the Soviet hit songs of the 1980s, and spoke about the atrocities caused by the French and the American people in Vietnam for more than a century. Yet, the French and American education systems were the ones my parents chose to put me through.

Where is the logic behind these seemingly illogical decisions?

The world was changing and Mom and Dad knew it. They knew it because they witnessed the fall of the Berlin Wall.

They knew it because they lived through the dissolution of the Soviet Union. They knew it because they belonged to the losing side and the view wasn't as nice. So, they decided to prepare my brother and I in the best way they knew how: enrolling us in what was deemed the best education systems available.

After all, they too had received the gift of the "best education" in their time and context.

That meant Phan and I would both enroll in a different school system than theirs, would potentially adhere to opposing schools of thoughts, and would eventually never see eye-to-eye, whether it would be about the best political governance or social inequalities. They took a gamble and experimented with their so-called most valuable possessions—*their kids*—to best prepare us for the world of the future: a globalized world instead of a polarized one.

With time, I finally reached that future state where I was definitely well prepared.

Or so I thought.

Thanks to my education, I was able to live in many different countries and continents around the globe and was in contact with many different cultures. Indeed, I benefited from the perks and advantages of being a weird culture kid. I could relate to many different cultures at the same time and see several different perspectives simultaneously because I never truly belonged to any of them fully, but only to fragments—*bits and pieces*—of them.

And that was why I had such a problem with the question "Where are you from?"—because I was not from anywhere but at the same time I was from everywhere. I found the question to be suffocating me because answering it by saying "I am Vietnamese" was never enough for me. I was from Vietnam because my family lived there, but I was ten times more eloquent in French than in my mother tongue. I was from Vietnam because of the way I looked but openly American in the way I experienced the world—*loudly and passionately*. I was the mosaic of every culture I had encountered and loved and, sometimes, even hated.

Perhaps we should start answering this question differently because for me culture—and by extension one's identity—was not necessarily where you lived, but how you've lived. Maybe next time somebody asked me that question, I would tell them about that time when I lived in Vietnam and ate spaghetti with chopsticks and Mom's phở with a fork. I could share with them my most traumatizing experience in life, when Mom always taught me that only kids possessed by the devil wore shoes indoors; whereas Kate—Tommy's Australian mom—made me wear my shoes indoors when I was at her place for fear of dirtying my little feet. Needless to say, I was convinced the devil had possessed me, and I cried for hours on end upon returning home from my playdate.

Mom laughed incessantly when she found out why I was crying. I was even more confused.

I had grown accustomed to those confused moments when I found myself between cultures and languages and rituals and customs, without belonging truly to any one of them. With time—*and a lot of courage*—I discovered that although I didn't fully belong anywhere, I belonged everywhere.

And that, ultimately, was my superpower as a weird culture kid.

Weird Culture Kids is a memoir of my growing up between different cultures from as early as I can remember until the end of high school. In this book, I explore the different confusing and oftentimes conflicting identities I've had growing up to understand how I've come to be the person I am today: culturally weird and eternally complex.

As part of my research, I have carried out more than a hundred interviews around the question "Where are you from?" with weird culture kids (WCKs) around the world, ranging from complete strangers to dearest of friends and family members. For this reason, several interviews with people whom I grew up with are weaved into the narrative of my book to give readers different perspectives of weird culture kids, along with a wider range of stories to relate to.

I hope you will find these experiences similar to your own laughs and heartbreaks.

This book is a tribute to the weird culture kids that some of us once were and continue to be. It is a celebration of all of those lonely moments in which we didn't fit in and of all of those awkward conversations that we couldn't enter. I invite you to not only acknowledge them but also embrace them, for these instances will sooner or later guide you through the sleepless nights of your identity quest.

Secondly, this book is also a tribute to the parents, teachers, and every single one in the support system of weird culture kids. Thank you for planting in us this curiosity to discover the world, sometimes with you and sometimes for you. Thank you for offering us such rich opportunities to experience life from such a unique angle and subsequently, for accepting us fully, with all the cultural weirdness we have built and forged throughout the upbringing we've received. Thank you also for your unconditional love and unreserved forgiveness for the countless times we blamed you for our identity crisis and our rootlessness.

We, too, forgive you for not fully understanding our cultural complexities and sometimes our multifaceted identities.

Thirdly, this book is also a teaser for all of you expats-to-be. I hope you'll love and hate your experience abroad as much as I did and still do. I hope you engage in weird conversations, adopt odd local rituals, and clash violently with the newness that surrounds you. Soon, these elements will be your norms. Soon, these will be the things you grieve. Soon, these will be the details you carry.

I hope each and every one of you will find shelter in these written words and a sense of community in these shared chapters.

And eventually "home" in this unusual book.

* * *

Weird Culture Kid:
/wɪəd ˈkʌltʃə kɪd/
noun - informal

Person who does not fit into any one specific cultural standard and who creates his or her own "weird culture" to give themself a sense of belonging. The process of making a "weird culture" is very straightforward: the WCK takes bits and pieces of the traditional and nation-state cultures previously experienced while growing up and mixes everything together to create their own customized culture. These customized cultures are deemed "weird" because, objectively, they have many different and conflicting elements within them, but somehow for the WCK in question, things just seem to fit and flow.

Weird culture kids were once children who grew up in international school systems or in foreign host countries and cultures. They were kids of international and biracial couples, and kids of immigrants who grew up in a place—*be it school system or country*—but didn't feel they completely belonged to the culture they were raised in.

Upon landing in the place commonly known as the "Real World" (for many, this "Real World" corresponds to their "official homeland," whether characterized by the passport they hold or the way they look), WCKs very often feel lost and uprooted. This is most definitely because they are grieving the loss of many elements at the same time: a city/country/continent or a culture/society/way of being, just to name a few.

For WCKs, their sense of home and belonging is not attached to a nation-state or a specific location. No, their sense of home and belonging is attached to (1) different people who also inhabited their multicultural childhood, (2) people who have gone through similar experiences as them elsewhere, and (3) countless moments—*memories*—captured within their overactive brains.

For the above reason, WCKs share a common fear which is that of the question "Where are you from?"

Once asked, the symptoms of this fear would be manifested in many different ways, but mainly:

- Mild anxiety
- Stuttering
- Overly elaborate answer that might make people think of them as arrogant and show-offish
- Overly curt answer that might make people think of them as rude and ill-mannered
- Answers changing according to the speaker and context leading to misunderstanding
- Conflicting and sometimes seemingly illogical answers

Ways to go around the issue and make a WCK feel slightly less stressed:

- Instead of asking, "Where are you from?" ask more pertinent questions such as "Where did you grow up? Where were you born? Which school system were you enrolled in?" and "What's your story?"
- Listen to their conflicting narrative
- Empathize

WCKs' customized weird culture and sense of not-belonging in today's nation-state paradigm will allow them to build an even more inclusive and more understanding world through increased compassion and shared living experiences, a world that transcends borders and nationalities by bringing the "us" and "them" closer together.

In the meantime, as all WCKs go through their own journey of identity-seeking, this book is proof that beyond their rootlessness, their tribe does, indeed, exist.

Here's a piece of belonging—*some sort of passport*—that every WCK can concretely and tangibly carry.

PART ONE

HOW VIETNAMESE AM I?

WEIRD FROM BIRTH

—

(Age 0 to 4)

My parents were Vietnamese Cold War kids who felt strongly Soviet. This sentence is weird to write, but it's true. Growing up in Vietnam during the Cold War period, they, like everyone else around them, had to choose a side embodied by a political ideology. Little did they know this choice was, by extension, also an identity they ended up strongly identifying with. Thus, just like that, the USSR's political ideology was the only one available and ready to receive them, given their Vietnamese nationality and passports.

Mom, a genius in my eyes, received a scholarship from the Vietnamese government to go to the USSR to attend the prestigious Financial Academy of Moscow and studied finance from 1972 until 1979. Several years later, she pursued a doctorate degree in the same university while she was pregnant with my older brother in 1989 and then with me in 1992. Her story is that of a girl from a very intellectual Hanoian family, whose determination in life was to get a stellar education abroad to later come back and help rebuild her war-torn country.

Dad, on the other hand, was lucky enough to be born into a rather well-off Vietnamese family. His own mother, my *bà nội*[1], was a very successful businesswoman of her time in Vietnam. She started out as a maid at the age of eight who slowly became the sole owner of one of the biggest chains of bakeries in the North and Communist part of Vietnam back then. Dad went to Russia in the late 1980s to work for Gazprom, a Russian gas production corporation, and the rest was history.

He met the beautiful and intelligent woman whom I would eventually call Mom. He fell in love with her, and she fell in love with him. Not long after, they founded a family.

A couple of years after the dissolution of the USSR, my parents moved back to Hanoi, Vietnam, a decision they consciously made perhaps not only to be closer to their respective families, but also to be further away from their disillusion with the system they so strongly believed in—*or maybe wanted to still believe in but no longer could*. That was the context in which my home was built. Dad was away all the time for business while Mom split her time between her day job as a banker at the State Bank of Vietnam and her night shift as the ideal mother she was destined to be.

My earliest memories as a child were in a huge Hanoian apartment, on top of the apartment of other relatives with whom I was never sure of how we were related but whom I always greeted with friendly designations like *cô, chú, anh,* and *chị* (Vietnamese for "aunty," "uncle," "older brother," and "older sister"). As far as I was concerned, everyone in my world was family to me.

---

[1] "Paternal grandmother" in Vietnamese

To get to my home, we had to walk through a pretty long alley, with the wall on the left-hand side and many different houses crowded on the right-hand side. Mom taught me to differentiate the right from the left here. I would walk that alley countless times repeating internally, "wall left, houses right," and the other way around when I walked out, "'wall right, houses left," always starting with the wall as a reference point not to get confused in my little mind.

After walking through that alley, I would reach a big patio always soaked in sunlight waiting patiently to welcome everyone inside. I remember spending a lot of time there with people slightly older than me, perhaps my brother's age, wasting time, waiting to grow up and be an adult. Very warm feelings always emerged whenever I thought of that patio. Maybe it was simply because that patio was always so bright and sunny. Our apartment was on the right-hand side of that patio on the second floor. A big and elegant wooden staircase led my little feet home, always, step by step. At the end of it, my favorite part of the apartment awaited: beautiful tiles on the floor, of different colors and motifs, changing according to the area of the apartment.

I still remember those tiles so well and vividly because I spent a lot of my time on them. I mostly lived on the floor in that apartment: I crawled on it as a toddler, played on it as a kid, and laid on it during the hot summer months as I grew slightly older. Maybe my little height pushed me to develop a highly intense relationship with the floor beneath my feet. Maybe it was simply the most beautiful and colorful floor I had seen in my entire life. Until this day, I still don't have the words to describe the bedroom's tiles, but I remember it was filled with both light and dark colored geometric shapes, aesthetically placed one next to the other.

A wonder in its own right for both kids and adults alike.

"These ceramic tiles date from the French period," my grandfather told me once when he saw me looking at them, mesmerized, as if I knew the French colonial history he was referring to in his words. As if I knew what "French" meant. I turned my gaze to his face, a beautiful face that embodied my definition of softness and kindness. I don't remember how I answered him, or rather, what my reaction was, though I didn't even think he was expecting an answer from me. He was probably just speaking to himself.

That was the first time in my life I remember hearing the word *Pháp* (Vietnamese for "France" or "French"). Slowly, this word would become so much more than just a word to me. Today, as I navigate life in my late twenties, Pháp remains forever close to my heart.

OTHERNESS

(Age 4 to 6)

Phan and I were among the first Vietnamese kids to be enrolled in the French international school of Hanoi. The small French expat community had opened the school out of necessity to ensure the continuity of their kids' education.

My parents, with strong recommendations of my French-speaking grandparents, enrolled the two of us almost immediately upon our arrival in Hanoi.

That was the beginning of my never-ending identity confusion.

It all started that first day of school, when Mom put a boiled egg and some vegetables into a Tupperware container and handed it to Dad. Dad then took my hand, along with the Tupperware, and brought me to my very first day of school. The walk felt like forever. I was dressed in a beautiful orange dress. I knew I was going to a place called "school," and I was going to meet new friends with whom I could play.

What I failed to understand at that specific moment was that Dad was not going to be there to watch me play with my new friends. No, even though I was very young, I knew that it wasn't a misunderstanding but that they—*the adults*—just flat out omitted to tell me that part.

Nobody told me Dad was just going to drop me off there, along with my Tupperware, and watch me for three seconds before walking out the same door that we used moments earlier to enter.

I actually don't remember how I felt. I just remember calling, *"Bố! Bố!"*[2]—but he didn't turn around. He just walked away while tears started streaming down my chubby cheeks.

I looked around me and had no idea what was going on. The world was so different from this place called school. School was very big and colorful, but I didn't think anyone lived there because I didn't see any beds or TVs. The floor was very different from the floor I was used to; the tiles were definitely not as polished as the one I had at home.

It just looked very cold and uninviting.

I cried the entire first day at school because I must have thought Dad had abandoned me. I cried so much that I threw up in the Tupperware container without eating any of my snacks. Finally, when Dad came back to fetch me, I wasn't angry at all.

I was just sitting there, doing something I now no longer remember doing. Suddenly, when I looked up, I saw him at the entrance, waving at me energetically and signaling me to walk back into his arms.

He acted as if he had never left me behind.

---

2   "Dad" in Vietnamese

And I acted accordingly.

Needless to say, Mom was more than surprised when she opened the Tupperware container filled with vomit that I carefully packed in my backpack and brought home.

"What happened?" she asked me gently, but I couldn't say anything and just looked down at the ground, perhaps a bit too tired to start crying again.

"It's alright baby girl; the egg just broke," she softly said, and I immediately flashed her a big smile thinking that I fooled Mom, the woman who knew everything about everything.

I don't remember any of the following days of school so it must have gotten much better. I must have understood the pattern: Dad would drop me off at school, then walk away to go to work. I needed to behave myself and stay in that new place and not cry (too much). I needed to make friends and play games and do activities with them.

At the end of the day, I would be picked up and dropped off on the welcoming tiles of my family's place.

Only then would I be left alone to play with the weird things I grew up with at home.

Among my most treasured toys were a bunch of different dolls nested in one another that my mom called *Matryoshka* ("Russian nested dolls"), but I just called them "Mummy dolls" because the former word was too hard to pronounce. These were "treasured" because they were usually on display in our big glass cupboard for us kids to look at only. I had never really played with them, ever. The only time I got to touch or interact with them was that first time when Mom brought them home and allowed my brother and I to take turns opening them up.

She was more fascinated by these dolls than us, that was for sure.

If I remember correctly, my brother and I didn't really know how to play with them and I don't blame us. How do people really play with those wooden round shapes anyway? They were called dolls but they didn't have hands or feet, so I couldn't walk them around the apartment and introduce them to their new friends. I remember within a couple of minutes of first meeting them, I had decided they were dolls for old people and one day, once I reached Mom's age, I would finally know how to play with them.

There was one small section of our cupboard that stored very colorful and cushy clothes that Phan and I never got to wear. Instead, we got to play with them. From time to time, we would take them out of the cupboard, lay them on the ground like we would with all of our other toys, and look at them.

After a while, Mom would eventually put them back where they belonged.

"These items are for you to wear when we return to Moscow," Mom would tell the both of us. I was confused at her use of the word "return" because I didn't remember ever being there. But I just nodded. At this point, I was about four or five, and I kind of knew what Moscow was. Through countless pictures, Mom had managed to give me an idea of what it was.

It was a faraway place from our home, and Mom couldn't take us there on her motorbike, like she always did when we went to *bà ngoại's*[3]. We would need to take a plane—*to fly*—to get there, "exactly like how we got to Vietnam a couple of years back," Mom would always say.

But of course, neither Phan nor I remembered that journey.

Moscow, Mom said, was that place in the pictures with a lot of white rain called "snow," huge buildings—*ten, twenty,*

---

3   "Maternal grandmother" in Vietnamese

infinity times our apartment!—and apparently the best ice cream in the world on Sundays. It's the place where you wear thick jackets and even gloves to shelter from the cold, a concept that Hanoians like myself were quite unfamiliar with.

Despite her obsession with the Soviet Union and everything related to it, Mom also raised us to be very Vietnamese. Every Mid-Autumn festival, we would always eat mooncakes together, some good and some rather disgusting ones. Mom would buy my brother and me all the traditional toys that kids usually received before going out in the street to join the festivities with all the other kids in the neighborhood.

The most memorable toy during that period for me was the *đèn ông sao*. The literal translation of this term in English would be "star lamp," which is quite an accurate description of what it was, minus the lamp part. Essentially, it was a star-shaped toy, made up of many different colored papers attached to a wooden stick, and the idea was for kids to carry these stars-on-sticks and walk together around the old quarter of Hanoi. Something like "we follow the stars because we carry the stars."

There was probably a lot of communist symbolism represented in that star and almost everything around me, but at the tender age of five or six, I just thought it was mad fun to walk around like that with strangers-suddenly-turned-friends.

Then along came Barbie into my collection of toys.

I shrieked the day Dad brought her home to me. I jumped up and down with happiness. She just looked so beautiful, I thought to myself. She was everything I wanted to become when I grew up: long blond hair, big blue eyes, and very, very nice clothes. My parents rejoiced at my happiness without knowing something weird had started forming in my head.

I struggled for quite some time finding her a name. Like most kids my age, I presume, I named my toys. But this one, I couldn't. I couldn't give her a Vietnamese name because she looked so different from me. She looked much more like my friends at school, and they were what we called *Française*[4].

As a rational young child, I decided to ask for my friends' opinion because they looked more like my Barbie than I did.

Some of my friends had blond hair, some had darker hair. Some even had freckles, something that I found super special because no one who looked like me seemed to have them. As a kid, I would sometimes take out brown markers and draw freckles on my own face; sometimes to look more like my friends, other times just to look different than everyone else.

My friends had different names than mine, names that I could pronounce, like Vera and Astrid and Emily. They, on the other hand, couldn't really pronounce mine. Granted, my name, Ngọc, was impossible for foreigners to pronounce because of the typical throat sound "Ng" that we have in the Vietnamese language, but I only learned that as I grew up. So, for many years of my life as a little human being, I was very shy when introducing my name to non-Vietnamese people because they would get it all wrong.

Or worse, they wouldn't get it at all but pretend they did and just go on without ever pronouncing my name.

I hated those moments because I felt very little every time I lived through them. So little, I felt invisible. So little, I felt like I never existed.

So instead of introducing myself as Ngọc, I became *Nioc*, a name I had to grow into, which eventually I learned to love.

---

4   "French" (female form) in French

I don't remember what the names my friends came up with to help me were, but none of their suggestions must have pleased me because I ended up calling my first Barbie, "Barbie," or more like "Ba-bi"—*with a Vietnamese pronunciation*—as I still hear my little voice call it sometimes in my head.

As time passed, I accumulated more and more Barbies in my collection of toys, and it got to a point where all of my other toys were slowly being replaced by these new and fashionable dolls. I wanted to be them when I grew up, beautiful and tall and elegant—just like how I wanted freckles on my face.

Writing this retrospectively, I realize I was learning to desire things I was never going to get.

DIANA MINH HẰNG DEEB ISHHAB: WE THE MUTANTS

For some unknown reason, Diana's Vietnamese name, Minh Hằng, was written between parentheses in her passport.

As if Vietnam as a country had to remind her, whenever she used her passport, she was only partly Vietnamese.

As if the juxtaposition of these different letters and sounds that made up her full name, Diana Minh Hằng Deeb Ishhab, didn't set her apart enough already.

I grew up calling her only by the name of Diana, as most people who knew her did. As a child, I thought Diana was much more fitting to her because of the way she looked. Minh Hằng sounded too Vietnamese for her. If she had darker hair, thinner lips, and whiter skin, she could have passed for a Minh Hằng.

But it wasn't her case.

Diana's stories revealed to me that external proofs of belonging—a country's language, mentality, official papers—had never been enough. The only element that could validate your own sense of belonging was yourself.

And, of course, the approval of the people you surrounded yourself with, whether you wanted that to be true or not.

Diana was Phan's close friend, and we'd known each other since a very young age. For many years now, she has always been the big sister I never had. Unlike me, she had always been the calm and responsible one. The reasonable and sometimes boring one (when she talked me out of my crazy adventures). The caring and nurturing one. I felt fascination toward her from a very young age and a tinge of jealousy when we were growing up together, exactly because of how cool I thought her to be.

Culturally speaking.

Diana was born into a very rare household: her father was Jordanian and her mother Vietnamese. Up until the age of eight, she was living in Syria—*a grander Syria, unlike the war-torn version of it that we often see on TV today*—and was speaking Arabic every day in both school and at home. She knew her mother was Vietnamese but knew nothing more about the country and its people, not even as a vacation destination where her family would visit during the summer.

For Diana at the age of eight, Vietnam was simply a country where people related to her lived, but she had never met them and could not communicate with them due to the language barrier.

And just like that, when she was about to enter second grade, her whole family moved to Vietnam to live closer to her mom's side of the family. Overnight, like many of the other weird culture kids who followed their parents around the world, Diana lost many, many things. She lost both big and small things, and she lost them in different rhythms.

She first lost the Mediterranean climate, a relaxed city, a familiar country, since these things were the most obvious external changes. Then, within days, reality taught her she'd lost a treasured friend, a favorite swing, a saliva-inducing dish. Gradually, she lost almost all the sounds she used to know, both ones she used to hear and ones she used to pronounce. She had to familiarize herself with new sounds that, once filled with meaning and given a bit of time, became words to her ears.

Upon landing in Vietnam, Diana immediately enrolled in the French international school where she found other people who were just as culturally weird as she was. So, she quickly learned two new languages, French at school and Vietnamese at home, while letting Arabic, her then mother tongue, take a secondary position in her new life (but still a primary one in her memories).

She found a strong sense of home in the *Lycée*[5] *Français Alexandre Yersin* because it was a very multicultural and international place, a place that shielded kids like herself from the homogeneous Vietnamese society that awaited her outside the green gates of the school.

"I used to think of our high school like the one created in the *X-Men* movies," Diana confessed half-jokingly, "because it felt like a place for mutants like myself to meet and socialize with other mutants. It felt like home, like a place to belong."

And that was Diana's vision of school as she was growing up because things were always simpler when we were kids. You didn't really notice differences and when you did, these differences were exactly just that—*differences*—with no judgment attached, and no side to take or comments to make.

---

5   "High school" in French

But when adolescence hit Diana, things became different. They weren't as easy as they used to be. Adolescence was never easy for anybody, but this time it was particularly hard for Diana because at that moment she had learned a bit more about herself and knew which type of people she wanted to be friends with the most: the Western-educated Vietnamese kids.

No one could blame her for gravitating toward them simply because she was them.

"Even though my dad was Jordanian, I was living in Vietnam for almost ten years already at that point. I was raised by a Vietnamese mother and was constantly surrounded by my Vietnamese family members," Diana explained.

She went on to confide how she felt closest to her Vietnamese-born but Western-educated friends because she knew they, too, had experienced the differences she endured. They, too, felt they had not completely fit in with the Vietnamese homogeneous society because they had been educated differently from a very young age.

And we all know how formative those early years are for any human being.

Diana didn't perceive any differences between her half-self and her full-Vietnamese friends because she had not only grown into her Vietnamese self (or at least into the definition of what the Vietnamese identity meant to her), but also actively chosen it as part of her identity. That was what she gained after losing so much when relocating from Syria to Vietnam.

Her sense of family and community had grown exponentially since she had moved to Southeast Asia with her nuclear family. Her deep respect toward her elders was now heightened since she found herself living in a Vietnamese home where several generations lived together under one roof. Most—if not everything—she did or said or thought was deeply Vietnamese.

Yet, she knew her friends didn't necessarily see her as fully one of them.

Vietnam, like many other Asian countries, is a society where you are either born Vietnamese or you are not. Diana fell into the in-between category because at least her mother was Vietnamese. But to Vietnamese people—the non-half Vietnamese majority, that is—Diana was considered to be automatically non-Vietnamese.

Or, at least, more of the non-Vietnamese part than the Vietnamese one.

And whether she felt that way didn't really matter because the most salient element about her when she first met someone was the way she looked: foreign. Her tan skin, freckled face (*freckles!*) and brown hair gave her non-Vietnamese identity away immediately.

Growing up, the typical scene in her social life looked and sounded something like this:

We would go to a bar together and she would order our drinks.

"Your Vietnamese is excellent," the bartender would always compliment her without hiding his astonishment.

Diana then either defended her *Vietnameseness* or, most of the time too tired, just paid for the drinks and walked away.

I, as her friend, never thought much about those moments because I understood that fully-Vietnamese bartender and knew I probably would have reacted the same way should I find myself in his position. Not out of meanness, but more out of the unusual situation he found himself in: taking orders from a Jordanian-Vietnamese girl in an expat bar in Hanoi.

That definitely did not happen every day. (Not to mention that the average person probably had no idea that Jordan was an actual country.)

In those alienating moments, she was grateful for being in the French international school because it was the perfect playground for people like her, thanks to the diverse student body it represented. In fact, whenever she felt too alienated from her Vietnamese identity, she could always find refuge in the French world—*or "other" world*—made up of the expat kids who also attended the school. There, too, she found some sense of belonging because Diana knew what it felt like to be an expat growing up in a different country.

Except that this country was supposed to be her own.

And that was where all the problems resided.

Today, as a woman in her thirties living in Paris, she confesses, once again, to feeling even more Vietnamese. Even after going through the whole French education system, even after living for more than a decade in Paris, even after acquiring her French nationality several years ago, her Vietnamese side was still the dominant one.

"Do you think that you will ever stop feeling 'other-ed'?" I timidly interrupted her with my question.

"It's a feeling so it's by nature fleeting. It never goes away completely and never stays around forever," Diana answered pensively while taking a sip of coffee from her mug.

"When does it go away for you then?"

Diana gave me a big smile. "When I'm with my kind of people."

(*So, choose those people wisely!*)

HOW VIETNAMESE AM I?

———

(Age 6 to 8)

My friends would always have to take off their shoes before entering my home, whereas I got to keep mine on when I went to theirs. My parents would tell me it's not at all hygienic to keep your shoes on when entering the house after walking around the whole city and amassing tons and tons of dust on them.

Mom would always say it was like "sweeping the house with a dust-filled broom."

In other words, not so logical or efficient.

"Is that so?" my French friend's mom asked me when I was having lunch at her house one day while I told her how my parents would have scolded me for at least eight minutes for wearing shoes inside my home.

"Yes. Mom says that only the bad kids do that. And I am not a bad kid because you have specifically asked me to keep them on, right?" I asked my friend's mom for her fiftieth confirmation to appease the need-of-approval child in me.

I knew Mom would disagree with her, but I was at her house now and I needed to hear her say I was, actually, a very well-behaved kid.

Over and over and over again.

She laughed and told me I wasn't a bad kid because I was told to keep them on. Then she added, as if noticing I was probably a little uncomfortable, I could take my shoes off if I so wished. I remember hesitating for a second but looking down at the floor through the glass table, I noticed how everyone had their shoes on. The kids (my friend included) and their Mom.

So, I shook my head, swallowed my mild discomfort, and told her I would rather keep them on.

Whether I made this decision to show her my adaptability or to unconsciously show her I was no different from her—and by extension, them—I would never know. With hindsight, I think it was a bit of both.

In my memory of today, that was one of the first cognitive clues that taught me to differentiate the two cultures, French and Vietnamese, that I was living in simultaneously. I repeated in my little brain, "French people wear their shoes inside the house and Vietnamese people take them off," just like when I was learning to differentiate my left hand and my right hand when I was younger.

When I was about eight, my friend noticed something different while having lunch at my house. "My parents don't use chopsticks at home," she announced her observation to no one in particular.

"You have forks and knives, right?" I replied immediately to show her how smart I was.

"Yeah, it's easier to grab things and I can eat more," my friend replied and laughed. I never thought it was hard to use chopsticks. Or at least, I didn't recall ever thinking that. It was all I had ever known. My parents used them and so did my uncle and my aunt and their families. Everyone in every restaurant was also using them. I knew that for a fact because we often drove past many restaurants where people sat on the street and ate all sorts of yummy things, with a pair of chopsticks in their right hand and a spoon in their left one.

Things my friends didn't often eat. Things my parents wouldn't let me eat.

But gosh, did they smell good.

Whenever my cousins were around, they would always ask me questions about French people. I told them they were very similar to us except they followed different rules than the ones we followed at home.

And, of course, they spoke a totally different language, but that I, too, spoke it.

"They use different utensils to eat at their home," I announced proudly.

"That's because the food that they eat is different from our food," my older cousin Dương took over the conversation. I was so impressed with her intelligence at that very moment. How did she know that if she didn't have French friends?

"Well, I can use both chopsticks and western utensils," I boasted, but everyone ignored me.

"What else? What else is different?" they urged. But I really didn't know what else.

"They are bigger than me," I shyly replied but my cousin contested that was because I was just a bag of bones and I didn't eat enough and went on about how my mom wanted to feed me more vegetables and milk so I could grow taller and bigger and stronger.

Like my Barbies.

We proceeded to play doctor and patient for a while, me being the patient as I was—*always, in every single context involving any single cousin that I had*—"too young to be a doctor." Suddenly, my uncle (although he was my cousin's age, our parental connection dictated that I call him "uncle") Tâm's eyes lit up and his mouth burst into uncontrollable laughter.

He shrieked, "I know. They sweat a lot more than we do. I know this French guy who lives not far from my house who is always soaked!"

Even though everyone burst out laughing, I didn't find it particularly funny. In fact, I noticed some sort of uneasy feeling within me—guilt, perhaps?—for laughing at people like my friends from school. I felt as if I was betraying them for some reason.

In that moment, I realized I felt a stronger sense of "us" in my friendships than in my kinships. Or at least I identified more with the French "them" than with the Vietnamese "us." I just thought that besides these more or less obvious differences—our height, weight, hair color—we were pretty much the same, my French friends and I.

We played at school and hung out at home. We chased one another in the cement courtyard. We climbed this mountain-like structure covered with nets at school together.

We shared secrets and swore to never tell anyone, ever.

Once, during recess, a friend of mine and I tasted sand together.

What an endearing thought to have: Somewhere in the world today lived a boy who once ate sand with me.

I wonder if he remembers my name.

ENCOUNTER WITH
A VIETNAMESE OF
THE ABROAD KIND

———

(Age 8+)

I was just going about my activities, like any other eight-year-old, when this weird little creature entered my world in 1999.

All of us were sitting on the ground, forming a circle—a big one!— while waiting for our new teacher to come in and tell us what to do. Since it was a new academic year, my extra-enthusiastic self came in early that day and took a seat on the ground, facing the two entrance doors of the classroom, one on the left and the other one on the right, with my back to the huge glass windows that opened to the main entrance of the school. I could have sat the other way, but my eight-year-old self back then didn't care much about the external world and anything that happened outside of my second-grade territory.

As all of the familiar faces started walking in, as we smiled and greeted one another eagerly, and as the circle started to slowly take the shape that our teacher intended it to be, in walked this creature who would soon become my bestie.

But, of course, our respective little selves didn't know that yet.

She came in and took a place opposite of me in the circle we were forming. I instantly knew she was going to be my "project." For that day, at least. Growing up in the French international school in Hanoi in the '90s, we rarely had new people coming in. In fact, not a lot of Vietnamese kids were enrolled at that time in the French school, and not a lot of French expats were coming into the country either to enroll their kids in the school that was initially built for them.

She was a newbie and she looked like me. Almost instantly, I felt the need to befriend and to integrate her. I felt the need to show her how things worked around the school, because I had been there since day one. So many questions popped into my head at that moment. *Did she know what she was getting herself into? Was she scared? Who was she?* While all of these questions were running through my mind, the door on the left suddenly opened and a beautiful woman with short hair and a very friendly face appeared.

The newbie turned around and with a perfect Vietnamese accent said to this woman, "*Mẹ ơi, con không sao. Mẹ về đi*[6]."

I immediately thought of the first day Dad brought me to school, but unlike this new girl, I never wanted him to let go of my hand. In fact, I specifically requested him to stay.

The teacher entered the class, and for a little while, it remained a brouhaha, like it always was at the beginning of

---

6   "Mom, I am fine. You can go home now."

every class. He also took a seat among us kids on the floor and we quieted down. As with every new academic year I recalled, we had to start the class by introducing ourselves to one another, as if he was afraid that over the summer we had either forgotten our French or built a new identity.

I waited patiently for all of my old friends to introduce themselves and tried to hide my eagerness to learn more about this new person sitting in front of me.

One more person and then it was her turn. I was ready to translate for her, if she needed help, I realized. After all, when I arrived to the French school three years before, I could barely say anything at all. So I knew what that meant and what that felt like. I was ready to save her and be her representative in this confusing world that was L'école Française Alexandre Yersin de Hanoi.

Her turn arrived and I looked at her with a huge smile, as if signaling to her I could help her translate her thoughts if she needed. I remember smiling so hard at her, a smile that was definitely too confident compared to the very little French I actually spoke at that point. But she didn't need my help. With a perfect French accent and a somewhat timid voice, she introduced herself:

"*Bonjour, je m'appelle Laurence et je viens d'Angola*[7]."

LIIIIIIAR! I screamed inside my head as she pronounced those words.

I didn't understand why she did that. It just didn't make any sense to me. How can she be Vietnamese and be called "Laurence"? She was supposed to have a name that was impossible to pronounce for French people, like mine. When she introduced herself, the teacher was supposed to ask her to

----

7   "Hello, my name is Laurence and I'm from Angola."

pronounce her name again, and again, and again. At least three times, to make sure the whole class got it. I would then offer to help teach everyone how to pronounce her name as correctly as possible down the road.

Where on earth is this made up country of whatever anyways? My head was boiling again and my heart was racing. Did she not know it wasn't in Europe, and Europe is only made up of France, England, Germany, Spain, and Italy? Why was no one calling her out on what she just said? Did everyone know what she was talking about but me?

I decided I was going to talk to her properly to understand what happened there. So during our 10:20 a.m. recess, I walked toward her to ask my questions.

Or rather, to throw my accusations at her.

"Hi," I said to her, with the authority and the confidence that only older kids would have on the younger ones.

"Hi Ngọc," she said while remembering and pronouncing my name perfectly. She smiled at me.

I hated her.

"Why is your name Laurence and why are you from that country that you said you were from?" I heard my thoughts pour out of my mouth without me being able to control them.

I didn't know why I was so upset and emotional about this new girl's introduction. I didn't understand either why my classmates weren't so preoccupied with the same thing I was preoccupied with. Maybe, unconsciously and prematurely, I thought she didn't want to be Vietnamese and I was exactly just that.

"Because that's how people call me at school and Angola is where I was living before coming here," she explained to me calmly and almost too nicely. Maybe she hadn't detected my dislike of her.

I decided to change my approach and softened my inquisition.

"But I heard you speak Vietnamese to your mom earlier, so how come you're not from here?"

"Well, my parents are Vietnamese and I think that makes me Vietnamese, too. But I've lived my whole life in Angola and have only just arrived in Hanoi a couple of weeks ago to live here with my mom and sister. So that's why I said that I'm from Angola."

"Where is that?" I asked, adding almost immediately, "That's not in Europe" to signal to her, that I, too, knew many things about the world.

"It's in Africa."

"But you're not African. Why were you living there?" At this point my mind was pumping out questions to ask this hated-turned-most-fascinating girl that I'd ever met thus far in my life. I wanted to write down all of my questions to ask her about the things she knew. I was excited to rush back home to tell my family, especially my brother, that there were people like us living in Africa, too.

We spent the entire recess session together, me asking her questions, her answering them patiently, one by one. She told me about her missing Luanda, the Angolan city where she had lived, and her friends, especially this girl called Sabrina, who had a swimming pool and tennis court inside her house.

"Is Sabrina like us, too?" I interrupted her story.

"No, she is French. Like most of my friends in Angola."

We had that in common, I told myself.

"I was the only Asian girl in school," she added.

Laurence continued her stories by telling me about her yellow toboggan and these specific types of chips called "fish croquettes" that she used to eat during her Angolan recess. She talked about how humid Hanoi was compared to Luanda.

I didn't really know what it felt like to live in a dry country, but I pretended to know what she was talking about, anyway.

Most of all, she missed her father who had to stay behind due to his work requirements.

"What were Angolan people like? Are they all Africans?" I asked

"Yes, they are black people. They are very nice and they have huge families. You know, all of my neighbors had ten to twelve kids," she explained.

"That's so big! How can you remember all the names of your siblings?" I exclaimed.

"Well, I can," she stated firmly. After all, only she knew the truth because she was from there.

"I had a lot of friends in my building and we would always play different games together. We had the sea next to us and lots of seafood. I just didn't really like the adults there. They always wanted to touch my hair and pull on my cheeks. ALL. THE. TIME," she continued.

"Why would they do that?"

"I don't know. I guess because I had different hair than their kids. And a different nose. And different eyes, as well. And all the boys in my building would tell me that they wanted to marry me when we got older," she added.

"Ewww." I felt a pinch of jealousy in my words as I answered my newest friend. I might have wanted the Angolan boys to want to marry me, too.

The teacher came out to tell us class had started again and we needed to head back.

"You can call me Thảo Hương, if you'd like. It's my Vietnamese name," she offered as we walked back to class together.

I thought for a second and answered, "'No, Laurence, I like your Angolan name."

We walked into class together that day, the same way we would walk in life together for the following twenty years.

TRẦN THANH THƯ: WHAT'S BEHIND A NAME?

———

"What's your name?" I asked her while thinking what an odd question to ask someone whom I knew so incredibly well.

Blindsided, she paused for a second and asked me, "Which name are you looking for?"

We both laughed and she instantly knew that I got it.

She arrived in the middle of fifth grade from Geneva, Switzerland, where her parents had just finished their term as Vietnamese diplomats. We met in class and instantly became friends.

First by default and, as we grew up, by choice.

The differences were remarkable between the two countries, Vietnam and Switzerland, which at that point, she had grown to know both quite well. Culturally speaking, she noticed upon setting foot in class on her first day that she was no longer the minority in many ways. She was no longer the rare Asian kid spotted in class among the majority of white classmates she had. But most importantly, she was no longer the rare Asian kid spotted in class who was carrying a mixture of cultures—*the Swiss and the Vietnamese one*—simultaneously.

She knew then that the other Vietnamese-born kids, myself included, were going through the same drill as she was and somehow that knowledge made her feel a kind of solidarity that she did not always feel prior to arriving in Hanoi.

And just like that, she started her life over.

The first element that changed was the way she was called.

"My parents named me Thanh Thư, which means 'delicate princess' and although I love my name, I think that it is exactly the opposite of my personality," she explained while laughing at her own observation.

I, too, loved her name. The way it sounded in Vietnamese was very light and flowy, and it had always made her feel very calm and composed. Her family name is "Trần." The Vietnamese "tr" sounded much heavier and the grave accent on it made the sound land pretty firmly once pronounced. Her full name "Trần Thanh Thư" was, for her, a perfect example of a well-balanced name: heavy and light, and solemn and playful all at the same time.

But while she was living in Switzerland, she was never called by her first name, "Thanh Thư," because it was too complicated for Swiss people—especially kids—to pronounce. So while in Geneva, she was called by her last name, "Trần," instead. It didn't bother her because she was too young to be bothered by anything identity-related. She was too young to understand the weight and importance that was packed into a simple name: Mere sounds at first, which later carried meanings and identities.

And in her case, solid and concrete memories of different periods of her life.

"Depending on the way people call me, I know exactly which phase of my life I met them," she told me, almost proudly.

"Trần" was her Swiss toddler identity. The few friends she had kept in contact with from that period of her life still called her the same way. Despite the decades that had slipped in between the her then and the her now, she still felt the same warmth and familiarity whenever she heard that name pronounced. She still felt some kind of belonging in that simple sound that used to be her name.

Especially when it was pronounced by gap-toothed Swiss kids.

When she moved back to Vietnam, the friends and people she met there called her Thanh Thư, some with the perfect Vietnamese accent and others with a typical foreign one, that of a French person with the basic understanding of Vietnamese tonality but still with the inability to produce such sounds.

While living in Vietnam, she always noticed these two totally different designations being used interchangeably. In fact, when we would be hanging out together—*French, Vietnamese, and all the other different nationalities combined*—everyone used the French accent and referred to her as "Tanh Tu."

This included her Vietnamese friends, who spoke fluent French and were very French themselves in many ways. Almost instinctively, they inherited the French accent while pronouncing a Vietnamese name with effortless ease. A friend could be calling her Thanh Thư with the perfect Vietnamese "th" sound or simply "Tanh Tu," the French way, with an aspirated "h" and it would all sound the same to her. Oddly enough, somehow, in that little international world of ours, these differences made perfect sense.

Both were her names and she identified strongly with them.

Moving from Hanoi to San Francisco was a totally different battle, not only because she loved her life in the French school in Vietnam, but also because she was at the age of fifteen and had just started to discover herself. Or, more accurately, the multiple facets of the self that she understood to be her.

And just like that, her parents uprooted her again and dropped her off, this time, in a public school in San Francisco within a span of two weeks. Within those fourteen days, many things in her life changed: friends, books, buildings. Language was a huge one. Her parents, for some reason, merely thought that since French and English were Western languages, she would have no problem learning English because she already spoke French.

What a reality distortion.

Almost like a tradition now, she had a new name. This happened mostly because Americans didn't use middle names, so she automatically became "Thư Trần," which never felt right to her. Additionally, maybe because she was never in contact with the American culture before then, her new community pronounced her name in a way she had never heard before. The light Vietnamese "th" sound was transformed into the "ch" sound and she now became "Chu Trân."

This bizarre name was too similar to both the train whistle sound—*choo choo!*—and the racist term "ching chong" for her to be able to adapt and relate.

To solve the issue, she did what she thought was the most American experiment to inaugurate her new life. She went to Starbucks and tested different names out at the counter. The act of grabbing coffee in the most quintessential American establishment and trying out different characters on the cups to see which one fit best felt so new and exhilarating. One day she was Rosa, the next Rachel, and the one after that Jennifer.

This experiment carried on every single time she would go to Starbucks, which was often. One day, an old name came back to haunt her. That name was "Ella," a character she invented in one of the writing classes she had back in the French school. Was it her subconscious nostalgia?

"What's your name?" the Starbucks staff asked her after taking her order.

"Ella," she confidently answered him, without any pause or hesitation.

In her head, she *was* Ella because she invented this character in a French writing class years ago. She suddenly felt like all the French authors who wrote masterpieces and created such complex characters and identities. These characters and identities came from somewhere deep down within the soul of their creators. She could now say the same. She could now feel the same.

She and Ella were one and the same.

I laughed as our conversation had dragged out a good thirty minutes just so she could fully explain her relationships with the different names she had learned to respond to and the ones she had consciously chosen.

We discussed all the different versions of her that I had met, whether it was the competitive Vietnamese-Swiss kid who was once my classmate, the fresh-off-the-boat Vietnamese girl who existed in San Francisco, the passionate hustler in New York, the startup marketer in Vietnam, or the nerdy accountant she was today in Canberra. I had met them all and had called her all of the different names she had had in her life.

We established that maybe—*just maybe*—she was wrong all along. Maybe the sound of the name didn't matter as much, but the voice that called it did.

"Where are you from, Ella?" I hesitated as now I wasn't sure how to call her anymore.

"Hanoi, Vietnam," she answered confidently.

"That sounds quite conflictive in my Vietnamese ears," I told her, "Ella from Hanoi."

"I'm just being pragmatic. Ever since I moved to the Western world, I have understood that the 'where are you from?' question is not so much related to my nationality but to my Asian look," she confessed matter-of-factly. And she was cool with that because she sincerely didn't feel like she fully belonged to any of these Western countries anyway.

"I guess belonging to people is enough," I added as if to console the both of us.

She nodded in agreement with me. She had told me over and over again that I was her time capsule, her mobile home.

And she was mine.

THE EXTRACURRICULAR LIFE

(Age 8 to 10)

Unlike normal kids, I hated summer.

As a matter of fact, whenever summer came around and my friends would go back to France to spend time with their extended families, I would stay behind to experience friendlessness in Hanoi. So the majority of my time was spent with my cousins. Some I grew up with, while others—many of them—just seemed to pop out of nowhere straight into my life.

Even though my cousins and I played together and laughed together and had some fun, it never was as much fun as I had with my friends. Come to think of it, the comparison wasn't fair because my cousins weren't my friends. They were at least five to six years older than I was and, thus, were going through their teenage years while I was still a small child.

Not to mention, at the age of ten, my command of the Vietnamese language was not good enough to fully understand their humor and enjoy their company. I was brought up to use the French language when speaking with my friends, while the Vietnamese language was mainly used to speak with my family members who were mostly my elders. That included my parents, my grandparents, and my aunts and uncles, and their respective kids. On this account, my Vietnamese was more than formal and in serious lack of cool slang to allow me to communicate freely with my Vietnamese peers.

Needless to say, I was not exactly the cool member of the crew.

Mom noticed my weak handle of Vietnamese—*or did she just notice I was excluded from all activities with my cousins?*—and subsequently took rapid measures: I was going to attend Vietnamese extracurricular lessons.

"Because you're not French. You're Vietnamese and you need to speak and write and understand fully your mother tongue," Mom firmly replied to my endless complaints.

Life changed in the weirdest way possible. The young girl I once was, who only spoke Vietnamese and not a single word of French, now spoke French much better than her own mother tongue.

And that was exactly what was keeping my parents awake at night and me awake during summer vacations.

When I was in third grade, I learned to communicate in French quite well. Or at least, well enough for me to have French friends whom I missed dearly in the months of July and August every year. But while they were away relaxing and going on awesome adventures, I had to learn Vietnamese grammar, spelling, and literature.

With time, "Vietnamese math" was added to my curriculum, as if numbers changed from one language to another.

Although my Vietnamese teacher told me on several occasions that I was bright, she hated my handwriting and made me feel bad about it every single chance she got. Naturally, she blamed it on the French education I was receiving at school. She said the French were not strict enough in the way they educated children and this relaxed upbringing was reflected in my handwriting, not to mention my below-average level in math, compared to the other Vietnamese kids my age.

On one occasion, I told my Vietnamese teacher we did far more interesting things in class than what she was teaching me at home. We didn't just do dictations and equations all the time. We read books and sang songs and performed theater. I got to be a sheep once in a school play. And in another one, I was a man buying some tickets at the train station.

"Well, but you're a girl, aren't you?" she asked me in a very loving voice, as if taking pity on me for receiving such bad education.

And with that, we carried on with Vietnamese grammar.

I don't know when the switch between my extracurricular French class and my extracurricular Vietnamese class happened, but I know for a fact that they never overlapped. They just replaced each other, naturally, as my affinity toward one culture or the other grew. My first extracurricular classes happened when I was around four or five years old, though they didn't feel like classes.

I was just in my study room with an older Vietnamese man, someone my father's age, who said things to me in French, and I was supposed to repeat after him words that I did not necessarily understand or remember. And with time, one day, I understood and I remembered. I enjoyed the classes thoroughly because the exercises were fun. For example, he would say different colors in French out loud, and I would subsequently choose the corresponding crayon and color the different squares he had previously drawn on my white paper.

Sometimes he would just raise a crayon up and ask me which color it was. I would tell him the color in French while feeling very good about myself. Slowly, as the years went by, I started noticing something I didn't notice before. Although I understood the French words he was teaching me, his accent was very different from the one I was hearing in school.

And this, he too noticed.

I had heard him tell my mother, on several occasions, that I didn't have any accent at all when I spoke French and this detail was like a badge of accomplishment that I carried internally every time I entered our study room. Then one day he just stopped coming. I didn't really ask any questions because his absence meant more free time for me to play with my toys and the new friends I was making at school.

My parents' attitude toward my fitting into the French world changed completely around the time when Vietnamese lessons were introduced into my life. I remember, when Phan and I were younger, our parents constantly encouraged us to speak with each other in French to practice it. Then, slowly and seamlessly, my parents' encouragement turned into annoyance when, out of habit, we would *only* speak to each other in French in front of them.

As I am reflecting today, almost two decades later, I wonder whether their annoyance and frustration actually reflected their fear of losing their children—or at least parts of their children—to a foreign world they never belonged to? Were they afraid their kids were becoming different people— *too different for them to ever understand fully*?

As a consequence and before I knew it, Vietnamese lessons were imposed on me.

First, I erroneously thought it was going to be as fun as my French classes were. Boy, was I wrong. I learned the strangest things in these classes, including how to hold a pen properly and how to write the alphabet with the correct handwriting. Other than that, the content was not necessarily hard because it felt like I was learning a foreign language that was my very own.

A lot of time had to pass before I finally understood my parents' seemingly erratic behavior, starting with their obsession with immersing me in the French world, which was later replaced by their compulsion to ensure that I was "Vietnamese enough." As we transitioned from one phase to the other, I often accused my parents for setting me up for failure.

How could I ever be "Vietnamese enough" if I was never immersed in the Vietnamese culture and literature and society like the regular Vietnamese kids? How could I ever be "Vietnamese enough" if I never attended Vietnamese schools and learned Vietnamese songs and made Vietnamese jokes?

How did one measure "enough" anyway?

I was not aware that, in their own traditional way, my parents were preparing me to deal with my budding feeling of rootlessness. They told me, on countless occasions, they didn't want me to be *mất gốc*, which is a Vietnamese expression that literally translates to "losing one's roots." So the Vietnamese extracurricular lessons were some sort of anchor they were offering me to later hold on to.

But I only realized this much later.

THE NON-EXTRACURRICULAR LIFE

———

(Age 8 to 10)

I didn't know what to do or how to kill time to make September come faster. Then one summer day, my Mom told Phan and I that we were going to have an older sister. It was as if Mom had heard my prayer.

I remember watching as Mom brought *chị*[8] to the empty room that would eventually become hers, on the third floor of our house. She must have told chị to make herself comfortable, to take a shower and to rest, before rushing downstairs to answer all of my questions.

"Who is she?" I rushed as I followed Mom from the living room, where I was waiting for her, to the kitchen.

"She's the new person who will be helping me take care of this household and of you guys."

---

8   "Older sister" in Vietnamese

"But doesn't she need to be in school?" I crossed my arms and looked directly at her.

"She left school a long time ago. She has to work to make money and to help her family out, so she will be staying with us from now on."

I still had many unanswered questions roaming in my head, but Mom had already left to do something else.

The next couple of months were wonderful because chị was around and we ended up spending a lot of time together. Her name was Thủy and I told her immediately that she shared the same name as my *bà ngoại*[9]. I introduced myself to her as Bi, the nickname my parents had given me from birth to be used at home by my family members to avoid confusion since Mom and I shared the same first name.

I immediately grew very close to chị Thủy because we were always home together and in many different ways, she was my first Vietnamese friend from outside of school. She was very patient with me and despite our age difference, she never made me feel like I was a kid in her presence. Unlike my older cousins whom I used to hang out with, chị Thủy liked including me in her activities. One of her passions in life was reading mangas. Every other day, she and I would go to the manga bookstore to rent out a couple of books to take home to read.

I remember countless evenings when I would find myself crawling into her bed just to read tome after tome of mangas, laughing about the plot with her and sharing with each other the beautiful drawings. Mom and Dad weren't particularly thrilled with this new habit of mine because they believed reading mangas would affect my eyesight due to the small print. When I pointed out it was probably the only thing

---

9   "Maternal grandmother" in Vietnamese

I was reading in the Vietnamese language, their previous remark suddenly no longer mattered.

I shared many things with chị Thủy and told her endless stories about the French school I attended and the different friends I had. She told me she had never seen a French person before. I promised her I would introduce her to some of my friends and told her they were all very nice. She told me about her family, back in the countryside and how life was different from the city. She talked about working in the rice fields before hopping on the bus to get to the city for the first time to come and work for us.

I asked her a lot about the games she would play with her friends back home, and she talked about games I had seen people play outside on the street but I, myself, had never played. She told me the boys would usually play *đá cầu*[10]—a very popular sport among my cousins and everyone around me, but it was never played at the French school.

"Don't the boys play football?" I asked her, wanting to discover more about life outside the French school in particular and outside of Hanoi in general.

"Sometimes they do, but the football itself is very expensive and we can't buy it in the village where I come from. So we would play football but with empty plastic bottles or tin cans. It's still a lot of fun, though."

I, too, wanted to play football with empty plastic bottles or tin cans.

"And the girls?" I pushed for even more stories and information. I was fascinated by this new creature, who, just like my French friends, was telling me about a totally different life she used to live, somewhere far away from here.

---

10 "Shuttlecock kicking" in Vietnamese

"All sorts of games!" she exclaimed while simultaneously peeling apples in the kitchen area. "We play different types of tag games. For example, a person was blindfolded and we would just be running around her to give her clues as to where we were but also to destabilize her. And if she manages to tag you, then you would be the one blindfolded."

She was a treasure trove of stories. I had never played that game with my friends before, but maybe I could introduce it to them when they came back in September.

"What kind of games do *you* play at school?" she asked me back, sounding just as curious as I was moments before.

"Mostly tag games and my favorite one is 'boys catch girls,'" I answered enthusiastically.

"Is it a fair game? Aren't the boys much faster than the girls?" chị asked, sounding very surprised.

"Maybe they are, but we are smarter. We don't take water or bathroom breaks, ever," I proudly proclaimed.

"Don't tell Mom and Dad I play these games though. They don't like me running around," I quickly whispered to her.

"Why don't they?" chị Thủy asked while giving me a very intrigued look.

"Because I fall a lot and look at all the scratches that I have on my legs," I replied while trying very hard to pull up my pant leg to show her my numerous scars. "Dad said that girls should never have scars like mine because I will never be able to wear dresses again," I recounted matter-of-factly while not feeling any kind of emotion toward my potential future without dresses.

And just like that, thanks to my new friendship with chị Thủy, my summer went by much faster than I expected.

School started, which meant I was going to be extremely busy, as I had to juggle French school classes, Vietnamese extracurricular classes, and a whole lot of socializing. My friends came back from their vacations with countless stories to share and I, too, was happy that I had stories to share with them because I had made a new, older friend over the summer.

Because the house I was living in at the time was atypically big, I hosted a lot of friend gatherings on Saturday afternoons that would sometimes last until the evening, when my parents would let me skip the weekly visit to my grandmother's.

At the beginning, I would tell chị to join me and my friends—*my French friends, I would proudly say*—but then I would notice how the ambience would get quite awkward for her because chị Thủy couldn't participate due to the language barrier. It was during one of the few Saturday afternoons that chị attended, when I asked myself, "Why didn't my French friends speak Vietnamese, and only the Vietnamese kids spoke French?"

I asked Phan my question one day, feeling as if I was betraying my French friends by what seemed, in my mind at the tender age of ten, like I was staging a coup d'état against the status quo. He didn't seem to think too hard on the question and just told me it was because they were French people.

"But we're Vietnamese and we speak French," I contested, which was immediately rebuked by Phan, who reminded me that I was in the French school and it was a requirement to speak the language, whereas it wasn't a requirement to speak Vietnamese to live in Vietnam.

I wasn't content with the answer.

As a matter of fact, I was even more confused simply because I didn't see the logic in it.

I thought if I was invested in the French language and culture—*even to the detriment of my own language and culture*—that at least they, too, had to make some efforts beyond counting in broken Vietnamese from one to ten.

I don't remember ever sharing these thoughts with anyone, for fear of being wrong and of not understanding the big picture. My parents didn't seem to be preoccupied with the fact that my friends didn't speak Vietnamese (as long as I did). They seemed to be sorrier, if anything, that they didn't speak French to communicate with my friends and their parents.

At the same time, Grandpa and Grandma spoke fluent French and went through the French system during their time as well. They didn't seem to mind, either. In fact, they were both a gazillion years old and if things had always been that way, then that was because it had worked well. I wasn't going to change that.

So as time went by, I kept my worlds separated: my French one at school and on Saturday afternoons and my Vietnamese one at home and on manga-reading evenings in chị Thủy's room.

FRENGLISH IS AN ACTUAL IDENTITY

——

(Age 10 to 12)

When I was in fourth grade, I was starting to get used to the fact that I didn't speak any language fluently, whether it was French or Vietnamese. However, I found a lot of comfort in the thought that the combination of the two languages was enough for me to communicate with the outside world the basic needs and feelings of a little child. I knew how to let people know when I was hungry or thirsty, hot or cold, happy or upset.

"The rest will figure itself out" was my anthem and self-consolation throughout primary school.

Around the same period of time, I recall my parents used to boast to their friends about my having foreign friends and the international world that I was living in. They frequently talked about it with pride and perhaps even a hint of envy, for they didn't get to grow up like my brother and I did. After all, they were and still are, Cold War kids.

How could they ever imagine that their source of pride and this constant international-ness was the thing that kept their little girl up at night, wondering what kind of world did she truly belong to outside of school, outside of the juxtaposition of kids from all different cultural backgrounds, outside of the bubble that her loving parents had craftily built around her in the name of love, progress, and globalization?

Between the age of eight and twelve, I stayed up very late at night wondering how to translate certain words from French to Vietnamese, or vice versa. Many nights, I fell asleep with a strong determination to be excellent in both languages. This determination grew simply because I naively thought my weak handle of both French and Vietnamese was the reason why I was deeply frustrated with myself and sometimes even with those around me. I concluded that becoming fluent in both languages would make my frustration dissipate and leave me alone at night.

To have a defined identity, I decided to be in control of the languages I spoke.

But sometimes—actually, most of the time—I didn't feel in control of anything at all, especially my language skills. I still recall the countless times when I have failed to express my needs or my opinions because I didn't feel equipped *enough* to do so; either I didn't know the word in the specific language I was employing, or I just didn't know the existence of such words in both languages.

Either way, I always ended up feeling rather stupid—stupid and lonely and misunderstood.

At times when I felt less ambitious, I would only pick one language, depending on the mood of the day, and decide to be the master of it. I desperately needed to find something to prove to myself that I belonged somewhere verbally, concretely, and explicitly. And that "something" that I had chosen as proof of belonging was a language—*and by extension, communication*—be it French or Vietnamese.

I was living, internally, within that context when I fell in fascination with my new friend, Tamara, and her family. She was the big sister of two adorable boys, Liam and Pablo, and daughter of a French mother, Claire, and a British-slash-Canadian father, Steve.

During my first time having lunch with them in their beautiful home somewhere in Xóm Chùa, I was captivated by the family's communication. Although French was the dominant language used at the table, the kids would occasionally throw in some English words, right in the middle of the sentence, while no one seemed to notice. Or even if anyone did, no one seemed to mind. No one even corrected them or told them they were using both languages at the same time. No one found it improper or accused them of not belonging.

Quite on the contrary, no one seemed to care and the conversation carried on. Most importantly, everyone understood the message. I felt something shifted within me during that specific lunch and as a kid, I remember thoroughly enjoying their company. These internationally mixed creatures made me feel whole and fully accepted somehow, mainly because they had shown me a different way to deal with the duality of the French and the Vietnamese I was carrying within me.

Maybe, these two languages—and by extension, cultures—didn't have to be so conflictive after all. Maybe, one day I could be just like Tamara's family: mixed creatures who wore their combination of cultures, languages, and ways of being proudly and confidently—much more like a beautiful ornament that made them unique, rather than a scarlet letter that alienated them from everyone else.

Without ever knowing, they showed a little girl how to embrace her very strange identity over lunch that day.

CHARLY WAI FELDMAN: ASIAN KIND OF JEW

———

"I have a Canadian passport," she reluctantly answered while looking as if she was being interrogated for a crime she didn't commit.

"That's not my question, though," I replied, amused at how offended her face looked.

After a small pause, she finally said:

"Then I guess I'm Canadian-ish."

Charly Wai Feldman was my friend from Vietnam, though nothing about her was Vietnamese, except that her father had been living in Hanoi for the last thirty years and that was where she grew up.

Charly was the daughter of a white Canadian father and an Asian Hong-Kongese mother. She lived as an expat in Vietnam from the age of five to the age of eighteen and attended the international French school throughout all of those years. Knowing her entire journey into adulthood, I knew exactly why the question "Where are you from?" made her uncomfortable.

Her go-to answer was usually Canada because her Canadian father had raised her and the only passport she has had until this day was a Canadian one. Not to mention the fact that she was one of the very few Canadian people who grew up in Hanoi back at that time and no one in the French school ever challenged her official identity.

Only when Charly arrived at McGill University, could she no longer just say "Canada" because that would invite people around her to ask further questions out of their need to connect: "Which city? Which neighborhood? Which zip code?"

She didn't have any answers to those follow-up questions.

"Whenever someone asked me where I was from, I would always answer something different like 'I grew up in Hanoi' or 'I was born in Montreal' or 'My dad's Canadian and my mother is Hong-Kongese,'" Charly confided while settling down comfortably on her bed.

Through Charly's personal experiences, she had grown to understand that most of the time, people asked her this question to try to determine why she looked the way she did.

She had never related to the Chinese culture because she didn't speak the language, nor did she feel familiar with it since she grew up with her white father instead of her Asian mother. On top of that, because she had lived most of her life in Vietnam, she automatically felt more Vietnamese than Chinese.

If the "Where are you from?" question was based on where Charly grew up, then she would have confidently answered "Hanoi"—"the Lycée Français Alexandre Yersin," to be even more specific, because it was in that environment where she hugely forged the person that she is today. She, too, felt French throughout her childhood up until her teenage years. She knew all the French cheeses—*from Comté to Camembert.*

She drank all sorts of French wine—*white wine and red wine and every-shade-in-between wine.* She'd read all the French classics—*ranging from Alexandre Dumas to Victor Hugo to later authors like Boris Vian and Louis-Ferdinand Céline.*

"What's funny is that despite me, I still get the most emotions out of Jacques Brel rather than Elton John," she shared, sounding rather melancholic. "For me, English is purely a language of communication while French is a language of emotion; English is definitely a brain-based and logical language while French is a heart-based and somewhat illogical one," her French side started to philosophize.

For a short while, we both indulged in our childhood memories back in our French school days.

It was there where we met and developed an ever-evolving relationship: Charly was first my dad's friend's daughter who I was forced to hang out with to practice socialization with white people. (*Yes, many Vietnamese people think that way.*) Even though she's a halfie, for Vietnamese people, she was automatically a westerner or at least some kind of not-entirely-us.

Then, as time passed, she became my English tutor because our fathers wanted us to be even closer. We didn't have arranged marriage in Vietnam, but we sure had arranged friendships. Through repetition, their tactics worked because with the passing of time we became friends—real friends now—and developed our own relationship independent of our fathers' friendship.

Whether it was because we just didn't have a choice anymore, because both fathers were very persistent, or because we actually grew to like each other, I couldn't really tell until this day. All I knew was at some point, and it felt quite organic, we became friends by choice and no longer by obligation.

At least whenever we hung out, I no longer took it as a socialization class with a white counterpart.

Charly was a very poised and beautiful person. I remember watching her during our family gatherings, speaking confidently about her thoughts and beliefs, expressing herself unapologetically. As I looked at her today, I thought she was exactly who she was always supposed to be: a wandering documentary filmmaker whose job was to share stories of other people while lending them her artistic eyes and her strong and determined voice.

If the "Where are you from?" question referred to a feeling of belonging one felt, then Charly would say she's from Jewish land—wherever that may be. In fact, the rootlessness she felt when growing up as a weird culture kid was probably one of the main reasons why she has identified the most with her Jewish identity for some time now. Jewish people had never been associated with a country and neither had Charly.

"It's weird how the places that usually invoke a sense of 'home' in me are never my actual home," Charly shared with me. "I once felt a strong sense of belonging in my uncle's New York apartment and later felt it again on my *Bubby's*[11] sofa. And most of the time, growing up in Hanoi, I felt at home only when I was driving my motorbike," she continued.

Another reason why she might have felt predominantly Jewish today was because she felt the need to express boldly and fiercely the minority element within her. She felt like her Jewish side was that minority she needed to nurture and protect. After all, the story of the Jewish people was one filled with resilience and perseverance, and those were the values she strongly identified with today.

---

11   "Grandmother" in Yiddish

Although she didn't identify fully with her Asian roots, there were certain elements in her understanding of what it meant to be Asian that were quite dominant in her personality. She was "Asian" specifically, yet neither Chinese nor Vietnamese, because those nation-based identities felt too claustrophobic to her mixed self. Feeling Asian was just geographically big and etymologically vague enough for Charly.

"I understand deeply the importance of 'saving face' in Asian cultures, whether I was in Hong Kong or Vietnam," she explained, "for example, I used to always fight everyone to pay for the bill regardless of who I was with because that was how people behaved in Vietnam."

We briefly spoke about how Asian societies did not encourage, in any shape or form, the practice of what the West beautifully called "to wear your heart on your sleeves." Charly, as a halfie, vacillated often between making her feelings transparent at times and burying them deep down within her in other moments.

"Is it hard to feel Asian and Jewish at the same time?" I asked her out of pure curiosity.

"Well, most of the time I find myself defending my Jewish identity exactly because I look Asian," she replied while letting out a semi-awkward laugh.

How horrible that must have felt, I thought, to have to defend your belonging to something you knew was innately yours.

In the same breath, she also confessed, "Though, my feeling predominantly Jewish has many overlaps with my Asian identity."

"How so?"

"Both cultures put a lot of emphasis on filial piety, which is the respect and support that one must feel and demonstrate toward the elders, especially one's parents and grandparents. And this sense of respect and support is something that I feel strongly in my life," she patiently explained.

Was it due to her specific combination of being an Asian Jew that this sense is heightened in herself, both consciously and subconsciously?

"Can you give me a concrete example of what filial piety means to an Asian Jew?" I asked.

I was extremely amused at the sight of her looking for an example as if she had something to prove to me, a full Asian person. As if she needed to forge her territory in terms of identity. As if the conciliation of her Jewish and Asian identities depended on it.

"Let's say that the idea of potentially having to literally wipe my in-laws' asses when they are old doesn't scare me. Like at all," she answered in a joking-though-dead-serious tone of voice.

I hadn't laughed so heartily in a while.

"You win, Charly. You win. You are definitely the most Asian person I know," I told her wholeheartedly.

If that was the standard definition of respect and support toward the elderly for Jewish people, then they, too, were much more Asian than they would ever know.

IT'S A "YES"

———

(Age 12+)

"He needs to feed you guys," the adults around me would always say, but I knew there was much more to it than just feeding.

Around the age of twelve, I already understood I had won the lottery and was born into a wealthier-than-average Vietnamese family. So for that reason, I always knew Dad didn't just work very hard to feed us. He worked very hard to feed us and beyond. To give us, my brother and I, much more than what we could have ever asked for at that age or at any age.

In exchange, we got to spend less time with him, barely any time with him.

The situation didn't change after Mom was diagnosed with lung cancer when I was in the sixth grade.

One day, as I was having yet another lunch at Tamara's house, her parents, Claire and Steve, unexpectedly invited me to spend a couple of weeks that summer with them in

France. I was crazily excited when I got the invitation, but I wasn't sure how I was going to ask for my parent's permission because I had never received such an invitation before. And just like that, after my playdate that day, Steve and Claire sent me home with a grown-up letter addressed to my parents to officially invite me to travel with them.

Naturally, the first person whom I asked about this was Mom because, traditionally, she was always the one deciding whether I could go to a social event or not; firstly, because she was the only one around, and secondly, because she was the more lenient one and tended to say yes to 98 percent of my requests. The other 2 percent of the time, she would consult Dad's opinion, which would always automatically result in a "no."

To be fair and transparent, the other 2 percent of the time was always the same request of sleeping over at my friends' homes.

"Why can't I ever sleep at my friend's house?" I would always bellow to whoever was listening to me at that time.

"Because you have your own house to sleep in," was the standard response I would get from both of them.

"But they get to sleep here all the time and I never get to sleep at theirs!" I insisted.

At this point, if Dad was on the phone answering my questions, he would have already hung up or asked Mom to speak to me.

If Mom was answering the questions, she would just pull out her I-don't-want-an-argument answer, "because darling, you're not French."

And that would be the end of the conversation.

So, to my utmost surprise, on that beautiful spring day, Mom said "yes" to my request to go with Tamara's family to

France. Almost immediately, as if she had felt my over-excitement and wanted to put an obstacle in my way, she also added I had to ask Dad for his permission, too, since it was a very long and faraway trip.

My mood instantly changed.

Growing up having Mom always available to me and taking care of me, I never thought of her as just Mom. She was also my close friend to whom I could tell everything and anything. Dad, on the other hand, wasn't my friend. He was just Dad. This is most probably because I grew up having him around only a couple of days per month, and thus I never got used to his presence around me and was pretty awkward around him most of the time. For me back then, Dad was mostly the voice— *literally, our relationship was very much phone-based*—of discipline who would decide things for me and about me, without really knowing who I really was and what I really wanted.

In fact, for some odd reason, I was actually mostly scared of him, even though he never did anything to me apart from saying "no" to my sleepovers. So when Mom told me to go ask Dad, I nodded but ended up saying nothing.

A few weeks went by and my dream of vacationing in France was over. I think I must have told Tamara that I couldn't make it because Mom was sick or some other excuse, but the reality was just that I didn't have the courage to ask Dad. Part of me was afraid to ask him while the other part just hadn't figured out what would be my most appropriate response to "But darling, you're not French" in case he were to use that argument, for lack of a better word, as the answer to my request.

So to make my life simpler, I dropped the subject.

And just like that, when I least expected it, one day when Dad suddenly picked me up from a friend's house after my playdate, he showed me Claire and Steve's letter that I had given to Mom weeks before and asked me why I didn't tell him about this. I didn't know why I couldn't look at him in the eyes. I felt like crying. As if I had done something terrible, I whispered to him, "because I didn't think you would say yes."

As if he realized the fear that he had unconsciously planted in me, he softened his tone and asked me if I wanted to go to France that summer. I still couldn't look up at him but instead, and I remember until this day, I stared at the backseat pocket in front of me. There was a stuffed box of Kleenex in it and I desperately wanted to take a tissue out to wipe away the tears I felt coming. I told him I wanted to go but I also understood if he didn't want me to do so.

"So you just assumed that I wouldn't want you to go?" he asked, trying to understand what was going on in my mind.

I nodded. At this point a tear or two had fallen down my cheeks and I was still looking at the Kleenex box, static as the car seemed to move faster and faster. I felt awkward crying in front of Dad for no apparent reason. I felt embarrassed to cry in front of the clearly uncomfortable driver as well.

"Why do you think that?" he pressed, softly with his voice.

I answered simply, "Because I'm not French and that would have been a summer-long of sleepovers."

He didn't answer or even if he did, I wasn't listening. I was focusing on holding back the tears in front of Dad while my eyes were fixing so incredibly hard on the black net of the seat pocket in front of me. I don't know how our conversation ended, but when we reached home, I ran inside to the bathroom, pretending to pee while aggressively wiping my tears away with the pink duck-printed toilet paper we used back then.

The next morning, as we were having breakfast, Dad gave me his permission to go to France for the summer.

I was finally going to discover what sleepovers were like.

Fast-forward fifteen years later, in yet another phone conversation between Dad and me, I asked him, "Why did you never let me sleepover at my friends' houses?"

"Because I didn't know your friends' families to entrust your care to them," he answered in a relaxed manner, as if his reasoning was the most logical one in the world.

"But you were never there, though," I wanted to reply but didn't.

Instead, I was surprised his answer wasn't "But darling, you are not French" this time. And that was enough to make the little girl in me ecstatic.

SUMMER-LONG
FRENCH SLEEPOVERS

———

(Age 12 Going on 13)

I was on top of the Eiffel Tower when I was six. Dad had
brought Phan and I to Paris for the first time that summer
because he wanted us to finally discover the faraway land
of France. Needless to say, the three of us loved Paris: the
beautiful architecture, the hustling and bustling activities
on the streets, and, naturally, the heterogeneous population
that made France, France.

Although I discovered many new things that summer,
what I found to be the most extraordinary was, without a
doubt, the French sun. It always generously stayed awake
all day long to make sure the three of us had enough time
to visit everything. You see, in Vietnam the sun had always,
almost religiously, gone to bed at around 6:00 p.m., which
also was the time our family would have dinner at home.
Yet, the French sun would go to bed much later, at around

9:00 p.m., like a naughty kid who refused to go to bed at a reasonable time.

I loved that sun.

These sudden flashbacks rushed into my jet-lagged mind as I sat in the van in which Claire and the kids had come to pick Steve and me up after our transcontinental flight together. I looked out at the scenery and noticed it was oh-so different from what I remembered of my earlier trip with my family just a few years back.

But I also realized I was different.

I was now older and more mature. I spoke much better French than I did back then. I could interact and be the main character of my existence in France rather than just being an observer like I was when I was six. Now, sitting in that van, I was traveling with my French and British friends, something I would have never imagined as the kid I once was.

As Claire was driving past endless empty fields of dry grass, my thoughts wandered to my previous trip to France. I saw in my head, flashbacks of the Eiffel Tower and of the Arc de Triomphe and how grandiose those French monuments looked from up close. I had never seen such big monuments in my life before.

Memories, memories.

The more we drove, the more my mind started to comprehend that, in fact, Paris was just a very, very small part of France and it wasn't representative of the whole country at all. The proof was that we had been sitting in this moving van for what felt like the entire flight from Asia to Europe and I still didn't see anything at all that I could have seen in my previous trip.

"We are almost home, Ngoc," Claire declared while looking at me through her rear-view mirror. "We rented a small house in this town called Malmont to be close to my parents."

Not too long after that announcement, we pulled up in the middle of a lot of nature—*the most nature I had ever seen up to that point of my life*—and in front of a small but beautiful house.

Being the city girl I was, I panicked. I wasn't familiar with any of this. There were way too many trees around me for my liking. And the grass! Too much dry grass everywhere! Not to mention there were a couple of horses we had driven past on our way to the house. I had never seen real horses outside of a zoo in my life.

Do they bite?

All of a sudden, I realized the France I was excited to find wasn't going to be there. It wasn't the France I remembered or believed it to be. Up until that point, I just automatically assumed whoever was French at school came from Paris. And by extension, everywhere in France was Paris. Boy, was I wrong.

I got out of the car, picked up my suitcase from the trunk, and entered the house to unpack.

Minutes later, I was back to my optimistic self because I noticed my favorite Parisian element was still here, in Malmont: I found again the loving sun I had longed for all of these years. The French sun was still as I remembered, softer than the Vietnamese one. Its embrace was never as hot or as aggressive as the one I usually got in Vietnam and thus allowed me to stay in its company for a much longer period. We all had lunch—or was it dinner?—together in the garden that day, with the sun giving all of us a welcome hug.

I've missed that hug.

To my utmost surprise, the following weeks were, until this day, one of the most fun and most educational summer vacations I have ever had.

I had to let go of my city life and adapt to a much more rustic one. Perhaps it was so educational because I think of those weeks as the time of my life where a lot of "firsts" happened. I first properly learned how to ride a bicycle. I remember the thrill I felt going down the hill on a bike, the joy I felt being balanced on two wheels for the first time, and the pain I tried to avoid at all costs biking it back up to the house.

I learned during that summer to go on hikes and explore nature, to swim in freezing lakes or any other bodies of water, and to pick raspberries or blueberries on the roadside for snacks. It was also on that trip when I developed a weird obsession for killing flies, or any other insects, because they were everywhere all the time, constantly.

The boys—Liam and Pablo—taught me this art.

"You see, Ngoc, this is a fly swatter," Liam explained as he handed me a tool that was essentially a flat plastic spatula.

"A what?" I answered thinking he was poking fun at me.

"A fly swatter," he repeated, looking amused. "You use this instrument to kill flies around here. Look!" he quickly pointed to the window and adeptly spanked the instrument on it. The fly's dead body subsequently fell to the ground. My jaw dropped while Liam's face was beaming.

He must have been very happy to teach his older sister's friend something new.

Gradually, what was once so foreign to me became part of the ordinary. With time, I ended up killing hundreds of flies, not just with the fly swatter but with just about anything, really, ranging from newspapers to flip-flops. The secret to this activity was speed and not so much the instrument.

I forewent my Vietnamese summer activities, which mainly consisted of staying in an air-conditioned room and connecting on MSN Messenger to speak with my friends who had gone back to France for summer vacation. Now, I was in France for summer vacation, but no sign of the internet was to be found, let alone MSN Messenger. Another activity that I would do a lot during my summers in Hanoi but not in France would be to binge watch *Lizzie McGuire* or *Sabrina the Teenage Witch* on DVDs while Mom was at work.

In Malmont, all of the time was spent offline, which was a very innovative way for me to spend the summer. I discovered the joy of reading as Tamara was a voracious reader. She read just about anything and everything. I, on the contrary, struggled with reading the foreword of just about anything mainly because I was used to watching things instead. I thought a lot about the different upbringing I had with my parents—mostly Mom—and the one I was receiving in France from Claire and Steve.

Mom, too, had encouraged me to read a lot growing up because she, herself, was obsessed with literature. However, all of the books she got me were Vietnamese books because she didn't read either French or English enough to truly be able to choose books of my taste. Not to mention foreign books in Vietnam back then were almost nonexistent, thereby adding another layer of difficulty for her to do so.

DVDs, on the other hand, were everywhere in Hanoi and simpler to choose from because Mom could easily just ask the shop owner for recommendations. Mom was never against me watching my DVDs hours on end because, for her, it was the best way for me to immerse myself in a new culture and environment. Come to think of it, my fluency in English today was highly thanks to the ten seasons of *Friends* and the countless episodes of Disney series that I was allowed to watch growing up.

Education in France was thus very different from the one I was receiving at home. In hindsight, I strongly believe it was due to our different cultural backgrounds. Just as Mom was trying to raise me in an international world—*one she never belonged to*—she had to use different tools to reach that goal, and her instrument of choice were English- and French-speaking DVDs for me to fully immerse myself in that global world.

Tamara didn't have to rely on the same tools as I did, for her parents were by nature very international. Her learning process of the French and English language was continuous whether she was in or out of school while mine was strictly divided between French at school and Vietnamese at home. I watched Tamara devour her books throughout that summer, pausing once in a while to ask her parents what a certain word meant instead of searching for it in a dictionary.

I, too, took advantage of Claire and Steve's language knowledge to do some shortcuts of my own.

Perhaps the most important lesson I learned in terms of cultural differences between a French and a Vietnamese upbringing was the degree of freedom the child got to explore the world around them from an early age. I saw that particularly as I watched Pablo playing. My parents had always encouraged me to play with my toys and dolls, but not so much to run around the garden or to participate in any kind of physical activities.

When I was much younger, my parents—especially Dad— were obsessed with my sweating. I remember not really being *allowed* to sweat. Every time I came home from a playdate sweating, Buddha forbid, I was immediately shipped to the shower by Mom and subsequently changed into a completely new outfit. There were days when I would change shirts three to four times, not because I was running around, but just because the Vietnamese heat was more powerful than my strong desire to stay dry.

Pablo, on the other hand, was allowed to do just about anything and everything. He was even allowed to climb trees! I remember once little Pablo was very upset at me because I would follow him everywhere trying to make sure he wouldn't get hurt. I would beg him to come down from a tree he was climbing, for fear of him falling down and getting a concussion.

In hindsight, I think he was a little bit amused at the beginning because no one had ever followed him that way before. But when he realized I wasn't playing pretend and I was actually committed to getting him down from the tree he was climbing, he finally got annoyed and informed me I wasn't his mother.

Pablo was right, I was simply being my own mom.

What surprised me most was that none of the adults really cared or panicked when they saw Pablo in a tree. The few times when he fell and cried for help, or simply just for attention, I was the only one freaking out, whereas Liam and Tamara would just carry on doing whatever it was they were busy doing. Seeing he was not getting the attention he was looking for, roughly ten to twelve seconds after his crying, Pablo would just stand up and go wash his new injury before carrying on with his day.

Later on, when Steve and Claire saw his wounded leg, they would only ask Pablo the simple question "what happened?" Pablo then proceeded in telling his own story—one that was completely different from mine—and it seemed like the ten-minute adventure he went through that morning in his own little world was so much more valuable than the fall he subsequently experienced. Just like that, after his story was done, the whole table would move on to the next topic.

No scolding from Claire and Steve. No babying from either Liam or Tamara. Just simple acknowledgement of what happened.

Like any kid being uprooted and then brought into a different culture for a while, I had to learn so many new things that summer: things I was taught explicitly, things I had to learn tacitly, and things I consciously or unconsciously adopted.

The things I learned that summer were numerous. Some I remember until this day—like how to play the board game *Mille Bornes*[12]—while others I no longer have access to the memories.

But what I know for sure is that I had somehow adopted, over the course of just a few weeks, a newborn confidence in my sense of identity, a hybrid between the different cultures I was exposed to and I was constantly interacting with. I decided it was okay to be a little bit of different cultures, languages, customs, and habits. Just like Liam, Pablo, and Tamara.

I didn't feel too alone anymore, for I had found my tribe: the tribe of those who lived between and among different cultures—fiercely, bravely, and authentically.

---

12   Mille Bornes is a famous French card game in which the different players are in a road race and the one who travels the farthest accumulates the most points and wins.

THINGS I KNEW TO BE TRUE ABOUT FRENCH CULTURE/ PEOPLE/COUNTRY

—

(Still Age 12 Going on 13)

Things I learned about French culture during my stay in Malmont:

- To say "hello" French people kiss each other on the cheeks. Sometimes they give two kisses (right then left), but other times they give out three (right then left then right again). I have yet to understand when they give two versus three kisses. Does it have anything to do with how much they like the person they're saying hello to?

- I had always linked the summer season with heat, but that was not true everywhere in the world. When I was in Paris at the age of six, the summer was very hot but still much easier to bear than the Vietnamese summer. However, some days in Malmont felt like the worst winter days of my life, especially at night. Those were confusing nights.

- French people eat a lot of different types of cheese that smell very interesting, but once you get used to eating it, you really get hooked on it. I am still unsure whether I was hooked on the cheeses or on the fresh bread.
- Vietnamese people, especially Vietnamese parents, would always force their guests to eat three to four times the portion of a normal human being—especially kids because all kids need to eat to grow taller (a very scientific fact, indeed). French (and British/Canadian) parents are not like that: If you're not hungry, don't force yourself.
- The French don't encourage kids to eat sugary food, including everything from Haribo to chocolate cakes (but I thought they make you grow taller).
- French women drive cars and vans. Throughout my trip, Claire drove a lot, and when we were on the highway, I saw a lot of other women driving cars and vans as well. That was very cool. Maybe one day I'll do that as well to impress Mom and Dad.
- Mosquitoes and insects love lights. Always turn off the lights thirty minutes before you go to bed and sit in the dark with your windows open. They will eventually get out and you will be able to close the window and sleep a bit more peacefully.
- Merguez sausage is life but so very spicy. Have a bite and a sip of water together.
- No bigger joy exists than a good chocolate and vanilla ice cream on a sunny day.
- French lakes are clean and serene, and you can actually swim in them.

- French people tend to eat a lot of green salads to start off their meals, which was my biggest nightmare. I hate eating leaves.
- They also love big tomatoes.
- Picnics and long walks in nature are actual activities and not just a wasting-time method.
- French grandparents are the most active grandparents in the world. Henri, Tamara's grandfather, drove us to town once and he was very old. The "classical music" kind of old.

I AM FRENCH TRAPPED BY VIETNAMESE PARENTS

———

(Age 14)

After that summer, not only did I feel more mature and comfortable with my rootlessness, I felt a lot more confident talking to the people around me, adults and children alike. My relationship with Mom and Dad also changed. I suddenly became more confrontational with them—*borderline angry*—and always demanded a concrete explanation or a logical argument to every question I asked.

Without really realizing it at first, I was slowly becoming more and more French. Or at least, more of what I understood to be French.

Looking back, I am convinced I turned out that way at around that time because in my history curriculum at school, we were studying the period of the French Revolution and the collapse of the all-powerful monarchy. Like most teenagers, I saw my parents as the biggest obstacles to my having fun and fully exploring life. At one point, I even saw Dad as Louis XIV, someone who I constantly had to fight against.

Mom remained my friend, but we weren't as close as we used to be when I was still a kid.

During those years, I did a lot of what later seemed to be things teenagers did. But for me, everything was so novel and exciting. I spent a lot of time with my friends lying on couches, watching movies, and wasting time. We talked about many things, ranging from books—*The Catcher in the Rye*—to series—*Friends,* what else?—to the older boys and girls and what was going on in their lives. I would usually eat dinner at home with my family although on nights when Dad wasn't home, which was most nights, Mom would let me stay over at my friends' and order pizza with them. She had always been the more lenient one.

Dad, on the other hand, was much stricter.

The first big fight between Dad and I occurred in 2006, when I was about fourteen.

"He said no?" I yelled as I yanked the phone from Mom's hand.

"Why not?" I yelled at Dad over the phone after not speaking to him for a few days already.

"Hello darling," Dad replied calmly, "because I said so," he continued while trying to avoid a phone argument with his melodramatic teenage daughter.

Composing myself and my thoughts, I matched my calmness with Dad's and asked him:

"Why can I spend a whole month of summer in France with my friend's family, yet I cannot be like the other kids who go and sleep over at their friends' houses?"

I just didn't understand why I was still the only kid not allowed to do sleepovers while everyone else in the world seemed to be doing exactly that.

"If I had known that sending you to France would make you so argumentative, I would have decided otherwise," he answered dryly.

I hung up the phone and ran to my room.

Phan had already warned me Dad was going to say no and I needed to make peace with it, but I didn't listen to him. I was convinced I could make Dad—or at least *Mom*—see my point of view. I wanted to share and engage them in my life, too. But as I was throwing things in my room that day and screaming random bad words in French because I didn't dare say them in Vietnamese, my brother just stood there looking amused and flashing me his semi-malicious smile.

I realized maybe Phan had gone the same route as me before and therefore knew from the get-go it wasn't going to work, and Dad wasn't going to change. My older brother had always been the trailblazer on the social and going out front. He had always been the one to push for a later curfew because he was older than I was and needed to go out to cool places that only opened in the evening.

Those were the places where I dreamt of going with my friends one day.

I had always admired Phan because he was always the cool kid among his friends. In school, he was well-known for both the good and the bad reasons. Regardless of what people said about him, I had always been proud of being his little sister. Growing up three years apart, we had always been close except from a hiatus of one or two years when I didn't exactly know what happened, but he became increasingly fascinated with his power to make me cry.

For an extended period of time, whenever the driver would drop us off at home after school, Phan would always rush into the kitchen to pull out a yellow knife and proceed in scaring me with it. By the time Mom came home, I had already lost twelve pounds of water from crying. When I subsequently told Mom about it, she would barely scold Phan because he was the golden boy and he would give me a look that promised another world of torture the next day.

Boy, was he messed up.

But we grew past that and now we had entered a new phase: the best friends one. I was fourteen going on fifteen when Phan taught me the real spirit of the revolution. The secret, he taught me, was not to ask Mom and Dad anything related to social events because they didn't know what it was like to be a teenager with non-war activities to do. We just had to do it.

I pondered on his words for a couple of days.

"What did you mean?" I asked him one evening in French to make sure Mom and Dad wouldn't understand what we were saying.

At this stage they still thought we were practicing French between the two of us.

"I meant that you can come out with me if you'd like. You just don't have to tell Mom and Dad about any of this," Phan spoke nonchalantly before adding, "I saw the girls yesterday at the bar and they asked about you."

Ooh la la.

I knew that because every Saturday afternoon I would call my girlfriends to hear all about their dancing and talking to new international people at all of these cool places that I didn't get to go. At that moment, Phan had already been sneaking out of the house for quite a while on the weekend to go party with his friends. He let me in on the secret a couple of months back, but I didn't want to disobey Mom and Dad. Or more like I thought I could change their Vietnamese minds.

But that was before I learned about Louis XVI and the French Revolution.

That night, I followed Phan and went out to join the fun the rest of the world seemed to be having without me up until that point. I took a deep breath and put on my high heels. Phan told me I should probably wear sneakers to be more comfortable, but I refused. It was going to be my big night and I had to come in with a bang.

"That bang is going to be the sound of you falling face first onto the ground at 6:00 a.m. when we come back home," Phan chuckled before expertly opening the door to his balcony without making a sound. That wasn't too far from what actually happened later on since our sneaking out adventure consisted of us having to hold onto a fence and then jumping from the second floor onto the first one.

I sure wished I was wearing sneakers at that moment.

That night was, and will always be, the best night of my life: I officially entered the cool grown-ups group. No one asked me what I was doing there or any other awkward questions. Instead, they just greeted me as if I had always been there, as if it was just another regular Friday night when we would hang out together. I entered the circle of Phan's crew and everyone was extremely loving and welcoming. I met a lot of kids from the United Nations international school as well and eventually became good friends with some of them.

I felt like I truly belonged there, among all of these grown-ups and grown-up wannabes, some I already knew very well while some I just met but instantly connected. Everyone took me in, offered me drinks, and by the end of the night, sometime between four and five in the morning, we dragged one another to the dance floor and just danced the last hour of the music away.

This was what Mom and Dad were keeping me away from, I told myself, while jumping up and down to the sound of intense dance music. They clearly didn't know of this place if they thought nothing good happened after 10:00 p.m. I learned that night that the best things in life actually happened *after* 10:00 p.m.: love, acceptance, and a whole lot of fun. At the tender age of fourteen, on a Saturday morning at sunrise, I told myself I wasn't going to *not* live my youth because my parents had forced their Vietnamese upbringing and identity on me.

And just like that, I danced into a phase in which I desperately needed to be French.

I was ready to abandon my Vietnamese identity and parents because I hopelessly craved the freedom that my French friends were having. They were the first ones to have Nokias with the snake game on it, but I had to use Mom's phone to text them and then subsequently delete the messages after—for fear of Mom snooping around my messages. They had pocket money to buy whatever snacks they would like and go for endless lattes at trendy places while I had to literally beg my parents to get me a bag of chips.

In reality, they constantly said no to my numerous demands because we were Vietnamese and that was how Vietnamese kids were supposed to grow up. And that was it. Nothing more, nothing less. Their definition of growing up Vietnamese was based on their own experiences as Vietnamese teenagers, which took place in a very different time, culturally, economically, and ideologically speaking.

But going through my teenage years with just "because you're Vietnamese" as an all-inclusive answer to all of my questions made me unable to relate to this forced identity.

"Why then, did you put me and my brother in the French school if you so badly wanted us to be Vietnamese, whatever that meant?" I would confront my parents at times.

Their answer was just as authoritarian as the Vietnamese political system, "Because you're only supposed to learn the good things from the French. Not everything from them."

My freshman and sophomore years in high school were a series of constant clashes between the French education I was receiving at school and the Vietnamese upbringing I was getting at home. It started with the little stuff, like "Why is Coca-Cola reserved only for special occasions?" or "Why can't I eat in my own room?" to the bigger ones, like "Why can't I go out past 10 p.m.?" which was usually countered by Mom's "Because that's when normal people go to sleep."

But I wasn't normal, though.

When things escalated, as they often did, I would be screaming, "Why can't you give me a reason other than your 'because you are Vietnamese' bullshit?" to both of my parents.

Firmly and immediately, they always countered with "We didn't pay for the French school for you to learn to answer your parents that way."

And they would always get the last word because they were my parents, the Louis XIV of the kingdom I was living in and to which they held the key to the main gate.

I started noticing my other Vietnamese friends at school were in the exact same situation as me, but they seemed to be content with their parents' rules and showed no interest in going out and socializing and smoking cigarettes and drinking alcohol with the rest of the French population at school.

The same went to all of my cousins and other Vietnamese people my age that I knew. They didn't seem to answer their parents the same way Phan and I were speaking to ours sometimes. My Vietnamese friends, too, thought my brother and I were a little bit too "Western" in the way we communicated with our parents: too direct and demanding compared to the communications in their household.

I didn't know how to think of the situation at that moment, since my Vietnamese friends from the French school were the ones I usually considered a fair norm, for they were also going through what I was going through.

I didn't understand why at school they taught us about the French Revolution and how important it was to question everything and anything—*especially the authorities*—and yet in life, I was barely allowed to question my parents. I asked Mom and Dad that question one day over dinner and received two totally different answers.

Mom, the softer and more compromise-oriented one, defended herself by saying she was always open to conversations with me, but sometimes, due to our different cultural baggage, we tended to look at things from different perspectives, thus leading to different conclusions and decisions. She softly reminded me I was only fourteen and at that age, she knew nothing else other than her school work. So with this being said, a 10:00 p.m. curfew for her was more than lenient.

Dad patiently waited for her to finish her good cop answer and jumped straight into the conversation, leveling up with the smarty pants teenage daughter of his: "Well, let me remind you that you are living in a Communist country and authoritarian regime. I adhere to it and would like to run my household that way. Any unhappy individual is more than welcome to leave and fend for herself."

As Dad said those words, I looked at Phan to give him a look that said, "Hey, we're going out tonight, right?"

Not long after I had this chat with Mom and Dad, I decided I was actually Française.

INTERVIEW

PHAN NGUYỄN: THOUGHTS OF AN EX-WHITE KID

———

Interviewing my big brother made me feel a bit anxious. I was looking forward to hearing what he had to say while simultaneously dreading it for some unknown reasons. I mostly wanted to know what his experience was growing up between the French world at school and the Vietnamese one at home. Unsurprisingly, his answer completely threw me off because it was nowhere near the identity I had donned on him in my mind.

Phan and I met each other in 1992 when he was roughly a three-year-old kid and I was a baby freshly out of my mother's womb. Since that day, Phan had to not only share a mother and a father with me, but also many other things in life. Like most siblings I knew, I assumed, my big brother and I had more ups than downs in our relationship. Despite our countless fights over the years, I remember he was always the one I looked up to the most when growing up.

As we conversed about our teenage years, I discovered many things about him that he had never shared before, not necessarily because he was hiding them from me, but because the opportunities never came up for us to discuss these topics. I realized throughout that two-hour conversation that although we grew up sitting next to each other in car rides to school, sharing a room with each other for many years, and fighting with each other over who got to eat the last piece of Mom's *bánh gối*,[13] Phan and I were living in completely different worlds internally.

Phan disclosed that for many years, he felt like he was a white French boy living in Vietnam.

"I think I decided to belong to France because the idea of it—*or at least what I understood it to be*—made me feel proud," he explained dispassionately.

I wasn't surprised to hear this from my older brother as I too had received the French education from as long as I could remember and had automatically inherited this pride from the get go. We realized that until today, we still regarded the French culture, poetry, literature, and everything taught to us in school as somehow better and classier and more elegant compared to any other nation's work—the Vietnamese one included.

But Phan and I differed in the fact that he felt extremely white attending the French lycée, while I didn't. Phan reminded me—and rightly so—that all of his references growing up about what it meant to be a teenage boy were very skewed and derived mainly from the American entertainment world. Movies like *American Pie* one to three hundred

---

13 Most well-kept secret of Vietnamese cuisine. If you've never eaten them, you should.

(how many were there anyway?) were what he imagined the norms to be and what he sourced his "cool model" from.

We had no Vietnamese equivalent of such coming-of-age movies and thus no one Phan could have potentially looked up to or imitated while forging his identity.

Besides, even if there were, the model that would be portrayed in such a movie would have been extremely different from the one that was his reality back at school. Phan explained to me how he initially started smoking cigarettes because he kept seeing those cool kids having coffees while smoking cigarettes every day after school at 5:30 p.m. He recounted the number of times when he wished he was one of those dudes in the café speaking to girls and being nonchalant about it. They looked so calm and relaxed with the cigarette dangling between their lips. They looked like they were having a lot of fun without him.

For some odd reason—*was it just his own self-pressure as a teenager?*—Phan desperately felt like he belonged in that group of white French kids. So he changed. He threw out his *Star Wars* T-shirts in exchange for colored polos because that's what those cigarette-smoking and coffee-drinking boys were wearing. He traded his brown khakis for those baggy jeans that covered only 12 percent of his ass when he walked. He even asked Dad to buy him Calvin Klein boxers whenever he traveled abroad because Phan noticed how the brand usually showed under his shirt.

"I was going through a makeover, an upgrade of some sort," he half-joked, "Just like MTV's 'PIMP MY RIDE.'"

I was glad he was able to joke about it now.

How cruel, I thought to myself, that a thirteen-year-old boy had to take the decision to consciously do a makeover to fit into the image of the cool kid that he so desperately wanted to be. Phan's definition of a cool dude was not only derived from the American entertainment industry, but also from the French white world he was surrounded by at school.

"The popular guys at school were all alpha males who spoke loudly, laughed nonchalantly, and always acted with confidence," Phan shared with me his "cool dude" formula.

In terms of activities, they didn't seem to read mangas like he did. No, they were much more sociable and outgoing. They smoked cigarettes and drank coffee after school and smoked cigarettes and drank alcohol at night. They walked slowly but fashionably to give people time to look up and admire them. In my head, I always thought those boys walked slowly because they were afraid that their jeans would fall off their legs. But what did I know?

Unlike Phan, I was neither male, nor white.

Phan had always known he was a sensitive guy—*hell, even I knew that*—and perhaps that was why he was so easily influenced. Flashbacks of moments when we would sit together and he would share with me his first CDs that were filled with classics like Savage Garden's *Truly, Madly, Deeply* or N-Sync's *Bye Bye Bye*. Later, when the MP3 era came, he was the one introducing me to Daniel Bedingfield's *If You're Not the One* and Ne-Yo's *So Sick*.

For heaven's sake, he was the original Britney Spears' lover with *...Baby One More Time* and *Oops!... I Did It Again* playing over and over again in our shared bedroom. And almost automatically, instinctively even, as his younger sister, I picked it up to impress him and to show him that I, too, had good taste.

I don't remember when the transition happened exactly, but soon I was the only one singing Phan's once beloved songs in our room by myself. Suddenly, he was too grown up to hang out with me. Suddenly, we just didn't share as much anymore. So he went on and liked different things and made new friends and started becoming this cool person he wanted to be in his mind.

Almost with a hint of nostalgia—*or was it regret?*—he explained to me how he used to like a lot of commercial music but the other alpha males he looked up to didn't, so they were the first elements to go to make room for his new persona.

"Do you really think that those songs we used to sing together are shitty?" I asked him, feeling almost hurt.

"I think I've brainwashed myself to believe so, yes" he answered.

Before I could even engage further to tell him how terribly wrong I thought he was, he looked me straight in the eyes:

"I used to pretend to like many different things in order to be seen as an alpha male because that was what I deemed cool. Over time, I found out that perhaps we were just a bunch of sensitive dudes pretending to be alpha males while growing up in order to fit in," Phan reminisced.

I nodded without really knowing how to proceed with this conversation.

He helped me out and added, "At one point, I forgot that I was just pretending and it gradually became real. And when things became real and I finally got to that realization, it was already too late to revert back."

Neither of us said anything.

"Despite my stories, I still like the way I turned out," Phan concluded while a self-satisfied smirk was appearing on his face.

As I am reflecting on our heartfelt conversation today, I feel a deep sense of gratefulness toward my sometimes-useless brother. I am grateful to have grown up with Phan because he gave me the Asian model of "cool" that he never had. I trace back all of the different moments in which I pretended to be someone who I was not to receive his approval and acceptance. In the end, I, too, liked the way I turned out.

And for that, I will forever remain in his debt.

PART TWO

HOW FRENCH AM I?

GOODBYE, HANOI DEAREST

———

(Age 15)

I never knew I couldn't just decide to be of a specific nationality, for there were way too many external factors and institutions that were obstacles to my decision. For instance, the most important obstacles were my parents, who also happened to be the people I loved the most in life.

How ironic, I used to think, that the same people who literally raised me with the motto *"you can be whoever you want to be"* were also the first ones to tell me I could not be French. I confronted Dad and asked him why he was smirking when I told him about my decision.

"Because it is just not a choice to be made, darling. You are either born into it or you're not. It's like saying Thomas was Vietnamese. That's just not true."

I thought about this argument for a couple of seconds and realized he had a point. I fired back, nonetheless.

"But you and Mom are part Soviet. How is that true?"

He proceeded to explain how a big chunk of his and Mom's life was spent there consciously appropriating the culture but also unconsciously soaking in Soviet customs and rituals and belief systems. That's what made them partly Soviet. Besides, he added in his adult explanation, the value systems between Vietnam and the USSR were extremely similar, since both countries formed part of the Eastern Bloc during the Cold War.

Everything seemed to bring us back to the Cold War with my parents sometimes.

I disagreed with this point and told him I was living in France at school, which was roughly 60 percent of my awake time.

That must mean something.

As if to appease me, he jokingly said I was indeed very French in the way I always answered my parents back. Well-behaved Vietnamese kids never spoke like that.

I was too tired to continue the discussion and also felt like he wanted to get out of it because he didn't think I made sense while I didn't think he was hearing me right.

I also remember for quite some time, I thought he was right. I didn't have anything to prove that I belonged to the French society, apart from my educational background, something that was so intangible and at times invisible to the outside world. I didn't have the most basic document like a French national ID card, let alone a French passport to tell the world I, too, had inherited part of their culture and history, and subsequently, a fragment of their collective identity.

Authority—*no, legitimacy*—was the lacking argument of my case.

A couple months into my sophomore year, my mind was preoccupied with something bigger and more immediate than my identity crisis: I had been accepted into an American boarding school in Connecticut and was going to leave Vietnam by the end of that academic year.

At this point, Mom was still fighting lung cancer and was living in Singapore where she was receiving her treatment, which meant that at home I was mostly living with just my brother and our staff. Sometimes my aunt would come by to say hi and stay with us, on and off, for a couple of days. Mom would come home intermittently from her treatment and most of our vacations were spent with her in Singapore, where she was hospitalized, just enjoying one another's company.

I was never worried about her health. A voice inside me told myself she was going to be alright and this was just a test she had to go through in her life.

Dad, being Dad, was traveling nonstop. So needless to say, in terms of our social life, it was indeed the best years of my brother's and my life. We would have a lot of parties at home, followed by endless nights of partying in the club and finishing on plastic chairs on the side of the streets to have a hot bowl of phở to sober up while watching the sunrise. Ten years later, I often still dream of that specific year of my life where there was never an end to having fun—the pure and uncontaminated type of fun.

At that moment, I noticed I had changed a lot. Ever since I'd experienced the grown-up nightlife, something in me truly shifted. I didn't feel like a little girl anymore. I started associating all the things I was doing with "adulthood": going out until dawn (although I still had to jump two fences to get there), drinking gin and tonic, and smoking endless cigarettes while debating the state of the world and other grown-up things.

I loved everything about that new life to the core, dangerously. I quickly became addicted to Marlboro Lights and have only managed to shake this obsession away recently as I am approaching my thirties. For many years, cigarettes represented such a huge part of my identity. I loved the way my brain would get a bit lighter every time I smoked and how the world around me would spin, ever so slightly, making me want to spin and dance with whatever and whoever was around.

I loved each and every conversation cigarettes had led me to. Sometimes they were highly intellectual ones while other times, they were just a bunch of harmless gossip. But they allowed me to create connections with others, taller and older and more grown-up others—a new demography I had slowly taken an interest in.

With time, cigarettes slowly turned into a symbol of freedom and adulthood for me. I, of course, had to do it clandestinely when I first started smoking and I told myself that the second that I would smoke cigarettes officially, only then would I be fully free and grown up. Of course, my parents didn't approve of it. Or to be more accurate, they didn't know about my newly developed habit to even approve or disapprove of it. But neither did Phan, at the beginning, which was an approval I desperately needed. After all, in my mind, Phan and I were one and the same.

We were both French kids trapped by Vietnamese parents. More importantly, I needed him to succeed in my own little revolution.

I remember washing my hands with sanitizer, spraying perfume all over my body, and chewing three tons of gum after every smoke break I took, whether it was in school or during the weekend. But it was all worth it. I learned to cherish those moments of resistance so very much mostly because they erroneously reinforced my French identity within me, boosted my defiance of the authority (Mom and Dad), and increased my contempt toward the establishment (Vietnamese culture).

And that was my life and mental state when I packed up my bags and moved to America.

JONAS PROTTE: FIERCELY ROOTLESS

———

Although Jonas didn't know where his next destination would be, he knew his departure was approaching. Soon, he would relocate again and again and again.

Jonas Protte was my childhood friend who had a lot of trouble staying in one place.

As a child, he was used to moving around the world due to his parents' jobs. Every four years or so, they would go to a different country with a new culture to start a new life. Jonas and his younger sister, Marine, would automatically follow. They would attend new schools, make new friends, and adopt new local cultures. Although Jonas still remembered the excruciating pain he felt every time he was taken away from his temporary home—*the overflowing tears, the tightness in his chest, the shortness of his breath*—he believed it was all worth it.

The proof was that he was still the same person today: rootless and restless.

But he was of the privilege kind. He was "rootless" because his sense of belonging knew no national boundaries, but his official papers still linked him to France. We spoke at length about his attachment to the country of wine and cheese. His conclusion sounded almost neutral:

"I am French because my parents are French, and so I inherited the nationality upon birth."

Generally speaking, Jonas was happy with what France represented—its ideals, values, and principles. But unlike more traditionally French people, Jonas didn't feel any strong sense of patriotism toward France. He wasn't blind to its flaws and imperfections. He never engaged in what seemed to be silly comparisons that involved pitting one country against another while using superlatives like better, stronger, smarter or any of their derivatives.

He didn't participate in that kind of debate because he felt like he belonged to many different cultures at the same time. Defending only France, he thought, was not fair enough.

It was not "him" enough.

"Why did you pick Bamako?" I asked Jonas about his current home, one that he had adopted as his own over the last four years.

"I was looking for a sense of familiarity," he answered plainly.

Despite his white skin, Jonas was (almost) a native of Bamako. He was born in France and moved to Mali with his parents when he was about three months old. Bamako was the place where Jonas lived for the first seven years of his life, right before he moved to Hanoi, Vietnam.

So when he packed his suitcase and boarded his flight from Paris to Bamako in 2017, Jonas had a plan in mind. He wanted to reconnect with his past. Jonas admitted he'd been feeling the urge to move back to the different places where he grew up for quite some time now because he wanted to reconnect to the inner child he once was. The inner child he continued to be.

What a brave move.

"Are you not afraid of no longer finding 'home' in those places?" I asked him, mostly out of curiosity but also out of jealousy because I knew I was still afraid to do so.

He flashed me an I-understand-your-fear kind of smile and confessed that his journey had not been exactly the way he had planned it to be. But it was and continued to be the best decision he had taken so far in his life.

The first time Jonas came back to Bamako since his departure in 1999 was in 2015, and that was one of the moments he would remember forever. It was the first time in his life when he was confronted with his past and his most cherished memories.

"You know, when you leave a place, you also leave a piece of yourself behind," he whispered softly. "To me, memories are connected to places, and they don't travel with me to the following location," Jonas described dreamily, as if these memories wanted—*deserved, even*—his undivided loyalty and attention. As if they, too, carried a nationality or were bounded within the borders of a nation-state.

So seventeen years after he left his first home, Jonas returned to it in a different body but still very much the same person.

A lot had changed and that was expected. Jonas described the house to me—"my house" he still called it—and explained how, within just a few minutes of arriving there, hundreds of flashbacks rushed into his adult head. He wasn't sure where these memories came from or where they were stored in the first place, but with every step he took closer to his house, a new memory emerged.

"I remember the trees in front of my house and how I used to play beneath them," he recounted before adding, "suddenly, they don't seem so big anymore."

That's because you're not so little anymore.

The new owners of the house took away the garden and put a garage there instead. But Jonas, somehow, still saw the garden in front of his eyes. He saw himself lying on the ground looking at the blue sky. He saw the grass that was no longer there, the bugs that have long departed.

"That experience has made my journey very much worthwhile," Jonas asserted, "because it confirmed my inner belief that as long as I don't go back to that place—*to my past*—I would never have access to the full memory bank that I have within me."

For Jonas, it was a no-brainer. He needed to get it back, slowly but surely. Sometimes these memories come more naturally and he didn't have to go too far to access them. Memories of the person he once was could be found in many things, but mostly tangible ones. An old piece of furniture could remind him of the way he used to sit, a familiar painting could prompt him of the way he used to feel, a specific smell could turn him into the teenager he used to be.

"When I was in university, I was very jealous of my classmates because they had access to all of the different steps and phases of their lives in the same place, people, and culture," Jonas confessed, "while I had to travel the world to get the bits and pieces of mine back, momentarily."

Being back in Bamako now, Jonas had also caught himself wishing he could have witnessed the evolutions of this beloved city, of Mali, of the African continent while growing up.

But instead, he moved to Hanoi, Vietnam, at the age of seven and blended right in with the melting-pot culture that was nurtured in the French international school. In the process, he became friends with other weird culture kids, which allowed him to feel "normal" for the five years he called

Vietnam home. Then he moved to Colombo, Sri Lanka, at the tender age of twelve, where he had to deal with his immense sense of missing his friends for a long time before finally integrating into the newness that surrounded him.

That newness had now become an integral part of him. A part he couldn't seem to shake off.

"The idea of settling down somewhere permanently really freaks me out," Jonas admitted.

"That's because you were never taught to settle down anywhere," I answered almost instinctively while thinking of his immediate family currently living in three different countries. "Or maybe you just haven't found the right place or person or moment to do so."

All Jonas knew was, for now, he wanted to continue to time travel. He wanted to go back to his past, to the different homes he had built and subsequently left behind. He wanted to move back to Hanoi or Colombo.

Or someplace new, even, but at least closer to these two Asian cities.

"Don't you feel like you're just frantically looking for something that you're missing from your past?"

"If that's the case, what's the worst that can come out of it?" he turned the question around before answering it himself, "some more missing?"

At that specific moment, I felt endlessly envious of his faith and zest in his own weird culture. After all, it's the journey and not the destination that counted right?

GOODBYE, PARENTS DEAREST

(Age 15+)

While both of my parents were sound asleep next to me on the flight to the United States, my mind tricked me into thinking I was about to live the life of the characters in *Gossip Girl* or *The O.C.* or even *One Tree Hill*. I imagined having a lot of cool friends and attending glamorous parties. Maybe I would even fundraise for some big cause, I thought, because that was what many American teenagers seem to do in the series I was watching. And they did so very successfully. Several hours of fantasies and movie scenes played in my head on that flight.

And oh boy, upon landing, both physically and figuratively, I had never been more crushed.

It was my fault for not doing enough research before getting there—to the kingdom of Connecticut—and that was completely due to the overly-positive side of me and to the

American entertainment world that I consumed every day. I wanted to be wowed by the grandeur and splendor and impressiveness of my new American life. I wanted to experience more joy and freedom and happiness, exactly like it was portrayed in American books and movies and series. I thought I was about to enter a foreign and more glamorous version of the life I was already living in Vietnam.

And I could not be more wrong.

The second I arrived to the place I was meant to call home for the following three years, I knew I was about to commit a very big mistake. Absolutely nothing of that new place reminded me of my actual home. The whole twenty-minute ride from our hotel in downtown Hartford to my boarding school was nothing like what I had imagined in my head. Nothing looked like Fifth Avenue or Times Square or any other place that had impressed me so much on TV.

Instead, I saw fields after fields after fields, which brought back very reassuring memories of my vacations with Tamara's family in the Southeast of France years before that. The fields here seemed less dry than the ones I had previously seen in Auroux and Malmont and Chastanier. But despite this fleeting reassurance, I still felt very foreign to this sight.

That cab ride felt long and unending. I suddenly started missing the girl I once was, some years back, sitting in that van, driving from whichever airport it was to our French vacation home. I needed her help badly at that moment because I wanted her innocence back. I knew she would have learned to really love the experience I was about to embark on if she was there because she didn't know who she truly was back then and was always down for an adventure to discover herself.

I, however, had changed from that previous self. In fact, the "me" then knew that after everything I had experienced in life, in adulthood, and in growing up, this culture shock was going to hit me like a bus. In fact, it had hit me already, over and over, as our car approached the elegant gate of the school.

I didn't utter a word to Mom and Dad because I knew it was too late for them to take me back to my old life.

Besides, seeing their faces flabbergasted by everything related to this school, I could sense how they seemed to wish they were students here as well.

"Look at this tree; it must be at least a hundred years old," Mom would exclaim while knocking at its trunk, as if to show Dad and I how old and powerful the tree really was.

"Look at the science building. Doesn't it make you want to be a scientist?" Dad declared while shaking his head as a sign of disbelief. His nerdy side was clearly awakened at the sight of the campus infrastructure.

I wondered if during that campus tour, they had started questioning their sense of identity that had so long been connected to the state of the world during the Cold War. Did their loyalty toward the Eastern Bloc waver when they imagined that several generations of students had been studying in this kind of institution instead? Seeing them so pleased and so proud, I decided I was going to let them live this experience vicariously through me.

So I swallowed my intuition and my first impressions of the school to join in the amazement.

Several days later when Mom and Dad had to take the plane back to Vietnam, I felt like I was that four-year-old kid again, screaming and begging for them not to let go of my hands. But this time it was different. They weren't holding my hands and I didn't beg them to stay. Unlike the memory I still had in my head of my first day of school, Dad wasn't so tall anymore, and Mom wasn't so joyful.

Instead, they were just two older versions of themselves, Dad with his shoulders looking almost too heavy for him to carry while Mom looking stern and emotionless in her face. Deep down, I knew she was trying very hard to hold back her tears. I knew that because I learned to do the same from watching her. Dad, on the other hand, was crying out all the water and orange juice he drank that morning. For a Dad who had not been very physically present throughout my childhood, I realized at that moment he was very much present whenever I needed him most. He might have missed my little and ordinary stepping stones, but he was always there for all of my milestones.

I told myself not to cry because I needed to be strong for them at that moment—*just as they were strong for me the first day they dropped me at school about a decade before that.*

And just like that, they sat in the car and the driver swiftly drove away, almost as if it was intentional so that they and I didn't have to live this goodbye any longer.

I didn't remember goodbyes ever being that painful.

DISCOVERED

———

(Still Age 15)

From the very beginning of my time in boarding school, I realized I was to unlearn and unsee and unfeel all of the experiences that had led me to that specific moment. I was asked, though never explicitly, to transform backward from being a young adult party animal who highly identified with French culture to being a simple Vietnamese fetus with no previous life experiences—because the ones I had accumulated didn't necessarily match with the school's values.

Needless to say, there was no smoking, no drinking, and no dancing, as I knew it. Study halls happened every night after dinner until lights out, which was around 10:00 p.m. I had to make my bed and clean my room, an activity I never learned to do while growing up with Mom. The school banned phone use during the week, and during the weekend when I got my Verizon red brick back, it was useless. I had no one to call except my older brother who seemed to be living the perfect Californian life as I had imagined for him.

I spoke English quite well by the time I arrived in Connecticut, but I wasn't fluent yet and was carrying around a very clear foreign accent. My accent was a mixture of all the international English teachers' accents that I had heard by then, from Ms. B to Mrs. G to Ms. M, along with the many British teachers I had when I was taking extracurricular classes outside of school to improve my English. This also included my newest Australian, American, and even Russian friends who I had made before leaving Vietnam. Their accents were also part of mine because we had grown to spend a lot of time together.

I was a beginner again, a beginner at this new life and new language that I was supposed to master.

My arrival in America exacerbated my identity crisis on many different levels because all of a sudden, I was no longer seen the way that I was used to being seen by the people around me. All of a sudden, I just became this international student from Vietnam. I wondered, what about my French heritage? Why were these elements not part of my introduction? How exactly was I supposed to incorporate them into my conversations when meeting new people? Were they even relevant?

Dad's words would bounce back in my head, now and then, to remind me my claims were illegitimate. I was hanging out with the few Vietnamese kids who were also enrolled in that school, and although we had a lot of very beautiful moments together, there were many bumpy instances.

Mostly ones in which I knew they knew I didn't belong.

I didn't always get a 100 percent of their jokes and they didn't always get my references. The problem was not "them" and "me." We weren't conflictive or in any way aggressive. We were just different and I, for once, didn't have any ally.

There was this girl in my dorm, though, who gave me a bit of hope from the first week of school. She was tall and beautiful and very foreign looking. This glimpse of hope ignited during one of our first ice-breaker sessions in our dorm. We were sitting around the common room, forming a huge circle, once again, like the one I used to be part of when I was in second grade with my teacher, Philippe. And one by one, we went around and introduced ourselves by telling everyone else our name, where we were from, and a fun fact about ourselves.

At this point, I was no longer used to these kinds of forced conversations or these ice-breaker activities because just a few weeks ago, I was still able to have what I deemed to be more adult-like conversations, whether it was about the American invasion of Iraq or the French colonial legacy in Vietnam.

My turn came without me even realizing it. I shyly introduced myself as "Ngoc Nguyen from Vietnam and my favorite series is *Friends*."

I hoped maybe some other girls in that room that day could also relate.

Before choosing *Friends*, I was thinking of all the French references I was used to in my old life, whether it was the girl band L5 or French rap—but that would have been odd for these references to come out of a Vietnamese girl, I told myself. Maybe even arrogant. So I opted for the more relatable choice. I didn't listen to anybody else's introduction after mine, whether because I was too busy day dreaming about my previous life in Vietnam or because I had already decided I didn't want to make new friends with anyone around me, I would never know.

Suddenly, a familiar sound brought me back to that awkward circle.

"My favorite book is *Le Rouge et le Noir* by Stendhal," she said.

Everyone around her looked very impressed by this girl's international dimension. I had no idea what her name was but was determined to find out because I had decided this French creature was going to be my friend. She just didn't know it yet.

I didn't care whether she was French in the traditional way or she was just French the same way I considered myself to be French. That didn't matter, I thought, because the mere fact of having someone to speak French with already made me super excited. So I started devising a plan of becoming her friend—in retrospect a little bit obsessively—and the hook was to let her know I, too, was somewhat French.

I still hadn't solved my problem of authority or legitimacy but thought things would sort themselves out.

My plan was useless because soon enough, on our first or second day of classes, I found her sitting in the same French AP class as me. It was a very small class with only six people, myself included, as it was the highest level of French in school. I initially felt quite bad for enrolling in a French class to start with since it almost felt like I was cheating, like I was going to get an easy A for something that was already a part of me. But a voice within myself told me I wasn't French after all and that was legitimate enough for me to enroll in that class.

That change of position within me, floating from my French self to my non-French self, was one of the most convenient traits I've learned to master over the years.

I was the last one to enter the classroom and immediately sat at the desk next to hers. The lesson started and I quickly realized it was mainly a grammar class rather than a literature one. It didn't matter much to me since I was desperately trying to recreate the ambience or somewhat the feeling I once had in the French school back in Hanoi.

On top of that, I was about to befriend the only French girl in school and claim back parts of the world I had just left behind a couple of weeks ago.

At one point, we had to explain in French to the whole class our answer to question 1.a., which essentially asked us to choose between *parce que*[14] and *puisque*[15]. The teacher asked me to share my answer, which I confidently did.

Almost immediately, the French girl poked me and whispered to me in French, "*Je ne savais pas que tu étais française*[16]!"

HOOOOO-LYYYYYY-SHIT.

I just got discovered.

I turned around, looked at her and acted surprise. "I'm not. I've just been to a French school my whole life. Until this year, clearly," I said nonchalantly although internally, I felt like I just scored the hottest date.

"Me too! I've been at the French School in New York my whole life. You?" my new friend asked enthusiastically.

"The one in Hanoi," I answered curtly while thinking that's what cool people did.

"Let's hang out," she said naturally and amiably before shifting her attention back to the lesson.

I felt an odd sense of relief and liberation at that moment because someone in my new school had finally seen me the way I had always been perceived, previously. We finally knew the same stuff.

---

14   "Because" in French
15   "Since" in French
16   "I didn't know that you were French!"

Most importantly, my goal was accomplished.

Although I still hated my new environment and life in general, knowing this girl brought back some kind of normalcy to my life. We started hanging out a lot since we were also living in the same dorm. She was on the second floor while I was on the first one. We shared different stories about our previous and respective lives and we discovered that although we were living thousands of miles apart before our encounter, our lives were similar in many different ways.

Firstly, the things we were taught at the French school, whether it was in New York or Hanoi were the same things. We had the same reference points both socially and academically. Secondly, we hated the fact that we were treated like kids again in this new school with every adult around us telling us what to do on a daily basis.

One evening, it must have been the second week of school, she told me to come up to her room after lights out because she had a surprise for me. I was more than thrilled. So around eleven o'clock that evening, I went upstairs. Every step brought me back to the time when I used to sneak out of my Hanoian home and climbed down the stairs from Phan's balcony toward freedom.

My new friend represented that freedom for me. As I knocked and went inside, her room was dark but she had prepared everything, like the rebel she was. A small bed lamp was plugged in on her desk and a small fan was also plugged in toward the direction of her open window.

"I got us cigarettes," she exclaimed, "and a bottle of vodka with some juices!"

I grabbed a plastic cup and joined her on the floor. Even though I had always hated vodka, the act of drinking and smoking in her dorm room that night felt normal and brought me a lot of comfort. I enjoyed the way the flame of the lighter kissed the tip of the Marlboro Light as I inhaled it in, as if taking in all the adulthood I had missed over the last few weeks. We drank and smoked that night until around three or four in the morning. We spoke again about the world outside of school and dreamt about the things we had yet to experience.

We talked about the things we would be doing once we got out, as if we were both inmates at a very privileged American prison.

"You've gone awfully far away from home to be imprisoned," she joked.

"There's no Wi-Fi in Vietnamese jails," I answered back playfully.

"There isn't here either," she answered, which was not totally untrue.

We spoke about the alcohol culture in the United States and how seriously the grown-ups took it. I thought it was the silliest thing in the world because that only encouraged excessive consumption by young people once they got their hands on a bottle of any kind.

"We Americans are an excessive people," she affirmed matter-of-factly.

I nodded in agreement.

Many stories and conversations later, I wished her goodnight and thanked her for the surprise. In the twelve-second walk back to my room, I pretended I was walking home from a long clubbing night in Hanoi. I even held my flip-flops in my hand to make the least noise possible, but the truth was, I was imagining they were my heels and my feet were too swollen from the intense dancing for me to continue wearing them.

She left boarding school a couple of weeks after that.

She told me she needed to leave for her own sanity. And that I, too, should just go back home, for she knew very well I was miserable, though the privileged kind of misery. Over those couple of weeks we spent together, I realized we were very different individuals. We hung out with different friend groups—*or at that point, acquaintance groups*—and only really chilled together in the evening over those smoking and drinking sessions that were occurring more frequently.

I realized we bonded in those moments because we mostly used that time as reminiscing sessions, both longing and dreaming about our past lives, ones we once inhabited. And now, she was going back to it. We gave each other a sense of identity that we both felt lacking in this new context. And just like that, she took off with a little piece of me that I would never get back while I returned to be the Vietnamese international student at an American boarding school.

Around the same time, my French teacher took notice of my sorrow and we started speaking after class. Madame, too, thought I was French and was wondering why I was taking this course. I explained to her my story, a story I had rehearsed hundreds of times in my head while waiting for someone else to ask me about it.

Just anyone curious enough to ask me a different question than "Where are you from?"

I disclosed to her my dislike of this new identity I was carrying around me, that of a Vietnamese international student. I told her how I really enjoyed the company of the other Vietnamese students in school, but yet I didn't feel fully understood. I told her I didn't know how to exactly approach the American students and how I didn't get the different cliques at school because my previous school was never big enough for us to be cliquey, and as a consequence, we were just one big, diverse group.

She listened to me patiently and I felt myself tearing up. I told her I loved her class because sometimes I did imagine myself being back at the French school and the thought brought me a lot of happiness. I also just missed speaking French since I no longer had a phone and my friends back home were mostly too busy having fun without me. She let me talk and listened to me patiently.

"Facebook is a good tool to stay in touch with friends and family, but it could also hinder your integration here because it gives you an illusion of being there in Hanoi while physically being here in Connecticut. So use it wisely," she casually slipped into our conversation.

I pocketed her advice like a used tissue and smiled diplomatically.

As time passed, I noticed I was looking more and more forward to our conversations after class and not just because I got to speak French again. No, there was much more to our exchanges now. I noticed from the very beginning that she wasn't treating me like a child, like most other teachers were doing. Instead, she talked to me like a grown-up and was genuinely interested in my world view. She shared with me her life story and how she arrived to the States from Paris and her marriage to her Italian-American sweetheart and her mixed-culture kids.

"I don't know what you're doing in Connecticut," I told her matter-of-factly.

"Where else would I be?" she replied, clearly amused.

"Paris," I answered, though I had never spent more than just a few days in the French capital.

We shared with each other many life stories. She brought me to her house sometimes to hang out with her two children who were a handful of years younger than me. I loved those moments because they really made me feel slightly normal again. I missed being in a moving vehicle that wasn't a school bus. I missed going out to places that wasn't a trip to the mall. I missed interacting with people who understood me genuinely.

I shared with her many stories from my previous and current life. I told her about all the troubles I got in at school. She didn't scold me and instead just laughed a genuine and hearty laugh, as if she was trying to tell me she was on my side and this whole situation was quite absurd.

But of course, she couldn't verbalize any of this since she was part of the establishment.

She listened, though, and did so without judgment. She listened to understand and to make me feel heard. And at the end of the day, that was all I ever needed. More than a drag of a cigarette, more than a sip of wine, more than any other external element I might be craving for at that time. All I wanted was to be seen and heard again.

And Madame did just that.

THINGS I KNEW TO BE TRUE ABOUT FRENCH VERSUS AMERICAN EDUCATION SYSTEMS

——

(Still Age 15)

French System (what I was used to):

1. The French grading system ranged from 0 to 20, but actually for me it was always between 10 and 17. A score of 20 signified perfection and was virtually never given because let's face it, we should only strive for perfection while never attaining it. Scores of 19 and 18 were equally rarely given, but I had seen and received a couple throughout my twelve years in the French school. Depending on the subject and level, a 16 was deemed an excellent grade.

2. "Excellent" or "Amazing" types of feedback didn't exist. They were usually between *Bien*[17] and *Très bien*[18].

3. The way the classroom was set up, students sat in pairs, with every two desks touching, and the teacher taught us distantly, at the front, from the blackboard.

4. Everyone in your grade—people of the same age—followed the same curriculum, and students were not allowed to choose their classes according to their strengths or interests. I really enjoyed this setup because it created great cohesion between all members of the class. Throughout the twelve years I was there, I had always felt very united with the rest of the class. The people who were stronger in a certain subject would help the less-strong ones out.

5. Sports was an interesting "subject" because we got to do different activities, including "circus." I never understood why "circus" was considered a sport.

6. I didn't know whether this was a French system thing or it was particular to my school, but the teachers would often come to the classroom where we found ourselves to teach us (instead of the other way around).

American System (what I was thrown into):

1. The grading system was out of 100 percent or five letter grades with each letter corresponding to a range of percentages, starting with an A being between 90 percent and 100 percent. A 100 percent or A+ grade was very attainable, as long as you put your efforts into getting it. I never found the classes or exams hard. They were just

---

17 "Good" in French
18 "Very good" in French

methodical and based on hard work rather than intelligence, per se. I absolutely loved this system because I knew exactly how many points were attributed to which question and what was expected of me to get full marks.

2. Whenever I found myself in the 90 percent range or above, "excellent work" would be written in big red letters on my copy. I took a while to get used to these very positive comments because I always expected lengthy feedback as to what I needed to improve.

3. Depending on the subject, the classroom's layout would be different. We often sat around an oval-shaped table—*the "Harkness table"*—in our English class. In history classes, we would have a U-shaped layout. Then in math or language classes, the configuration of the classroom would be very similar to what I was used to in the French school, but the rows were made of individual tables instead of pairs.

4. Once the core requirements were fulfilled, you were free to choose the classes that interested you most. Additionally, you would be placed in different language, math, and science classes depending on your level of performance in each of these subjects. Although I thought this level of customization was great for my learning abilities, I didn't necessarily think it helped me form solid friendships through classes.

5. There were serious sports teams in my school. I even joined the softball team. Every other Saturday, we would travel to other schools to compete. The Americans really took sports to the next level. Later on, I understood the importance of having good sports team in high schools because "sports scholarship" was a huge thing in the United States.

6. The teachers had assigned classrooms, so the students needed to move from one place to the other to attend their scheduled classes.

Most of the time when I would get into the subject of education systems with my French friends, the conversation would get quite tense—something I learned to be comfortable with. As I had the chance to experience both systems, I felt the French grading system was setting me up for failure, since the best grade, 20, was virtually unattainable.

Naturally, my comment was met with a lot of pushback. We would proceed in talking about the "easy" grading system in American schools. And as if the comparison between the two grading systems was not big enough of a subject, we overflowed onto the grander theme of cultures and how these scales were highly culturally dependent.

They attacked the American grading system for being inflated because Americans found everything to be *amazing and fantastic and awesome.*" Meanwhile, taking these comments very personally, I asserted the French grading system promised its students the impossible and in turn conditioned the students who came out of this system to be unsatisfied with almost everything that ever existed. This was seen, according to my view, with the everyday expressions like *c'est pas terrible*[19] to describe something of medium quality and *c'est pas mal*[20] to describe a positive experience.

We couldn't have chosen two more opposite cultures.

We never reached any conclusion regarding this specific point, but it stayed with me for a while because it was the first time where I felt "othered" by the people whom I had always considered to be 100 percent like myself.

Worse, I felt proudly American.

---

19   "It's not terrible" in French
20   "It's not bad" in French

MAI NGUYỄN: ULTIMATELY HOME

———

I dialed Mai's British number from my French phone and within seconds, I heard her familiar "hello?" coming into my Parisian living room.

As usual, she was living her expat life in a foreign country. Unusually, though, this time her expatriation was of her own choosing. She consciously chose London.

These cool Vietnamese kids from abroad started to enter my life in elementary school and Mai was one of them. They fascinated me, these Vietnamese-looking kids who, like my French friends in Vietnam, only came and stayed for a few years before packing their bags again to start a new adventure with their family someplace else.

With time, I understood that these Vietnamese children were the "embassy kids" because they grew up in different Vietnamese embassies around the world. Their parents were Vietnamese diplomats, which explained why they'd traveled so much and were so worldly from a very young age. Yet, they were still strongly connected to Vietnam because they were raised in the Vietnamese embassies, which were technically Vietnamese soil but abroad.

As a consequence—*or was it a side effect?*—of this type of upbringing, these kids were, from a young age, professional expats.

Sadly, even expats in their own home country sometimes.

"It wasn't always easy when I was growing up," Mai confessed during our interview, "because it felt as if there was an additional layer of difficulty when I was a child and then teenager."

As Mai navigated through the different worlds offered in local and international schools of various countries, she observed, with hindsight, that her lifestyle was more fitting in the international school environment rather than a local one. With time—a lot of time—it became apparent that Mai didn't have the lifestyle the majority of the children in the world were having: a more stable and rooted one.

Before attending the French international school in Hanoi at the age of nine, Mai was living her ordinary life as an embassy kid in Geneva, Switzerland. And like all of the neighboring kids, she attended the Swiss local kindergarten and later primary school. When Mai entered third grade, she moved to Hanoi and became my friend for four years.

The realization that her life was a bit weirder than that of the average kid only emerged in her mind when she returned to Switzerland the second time to resume her life as an embassy kid.

Upon her coming back to Geneva, Mai immediately noticed something was out of her ordinary, out of her normalcy. The same kids who were in her kindergarten were still there. Exactly how Mai had left them, except they had grown taller. And not only were they still there, they were also still friends with each other. Exactly like how she remembered them.

This simple realization highlighted the stability that Mai never had. Inevitably, this thought made her feel like she was the odd one out, not only because she was the newest member of the class (maybe even the *only* new member of that class), but also because she couldn't relate to any of her peers.

She couldn't relate to them because she was too different from them.

"I had no idea what it was like to live in the same place for more than four years growing up. And at that age, four years seemed like forever already," Mai confessed earnestly.

Not to mention that Mai didn't even know what it felt like to attend the same school system throughout her whole academic life because she had just been vacillating between a Swiss system and a French one over the years. Most importantly, she didn't know what it felt like to benefit from the comfort of being surrounded by the same people since her early ages because, naturally, due to Mai's frequent relocations, her friendships were mostly characterized by distance and the struggle of maintaining contact.

Sometimes, the most important distance that separated her from her friends was time itself.

She confessed to resent her lifestyle on more than one occasion. She still remembered how difficult and challenging every relocation was for her. How much she dreaded that first day of class in a new school.

She recounted her first memory of being in her Swiss kindergarten and not being able to communicate with anyone because she didn't speak French. What added to her frustration was her inability to understand what was going on around her in class. I wonder whether that abrupt change of language, along with the major change in environment, had made Mai, throughout her younger years, a very shy and introverted kid.

"Did you have the same feeling when you entered our French school in Hanoi?" I asked her because I had always remembered Mai as a timid kid throughout our Hanoian years.

"A somewhat similar feeling but less salient," Mai confirmed. "It was similar because I was also entering a very tight-knit community of kids who had known each other for quite some time already," she added.

I thought it was more of a projection of her previous experience because I remembered the class "turnover" to be pretty high. After all, it was essentially a school for expat kids, and "expat" was synonymous with "temporary." But I also remembered how tight we all were. How it felt like we were all one family, due to the small class size.

And that mere fact, objectively, could be quite daunting for a newcomer.

Mai explained that, growing up, she often found it very difficult to make friends because of the shy person she somehow was. She had a lot of things on her mind, a lot of ideas and opinions, but somehow she couldn't express them to the outside world.

If you knew Mai today, you would immediately notice that nothing about her—*from the way she talks to the way she carries herself*—would lead you to think this girl was once the shyest girl ever.

"What do you think happened?" I interrupted.

"London happened," Mai answered enigmatically, as she looked at me on her phone and walked across the park to get to the tube station.

Mai had been living in London for the past ten years and had credited this city for a huge part of her "becoming" process. London was a very diverse and international city, which was a perfect fit for Mai's multicultural dimension. Ever since arriving in London, Mai didn't feel like she needed to fit into any cultural norms or standards anymore. Upon landing in London for university, she instantly understood that she didn't have to say certain things or act a certain way for people to like her.

London was the first place that allowed her to be herself, truly and fiercely so. London was the first place that fully liked and accepted her. Most importantly, London was the first place that allowed Mai to finally explore all of the different cultures she had previously come into contact with to shape the person she was today. For the first time, Mai didn't feel the need to box herself into any one specific persona or culture or nationality to feel welcomed in a place.

"I love my experience in London so much most probably because it wasn't imposed on me," Mai shared genuinely, "It was the first relocation that I did out of choice and not out of obligation."

This mere fact changed everything.

We continued our interview-turned-hang-out session very casually. We compared the French education system with the Anglophone one. We exchanged stories about our respective experiences studying International Relations in our bachelor years. Mai told me the people she met in London studying IR were exactly like her: culturally weird yet incredibly interesting. Their points of view were original and oftentimes conflicting.

"I'm not surprised," I answered mischievously and we both laughed the I-know-what-you-mean kind of laugh.

As we wrapped up our conversation, I asked Mai whether she felt like she belonged somehow while being enrolled in the French school in Hanoi.

"I was too young to understand that I could have belonged in a way or another; that there existed even different ways to belong," Mai finally let out after a short pause. She continued by explaining it would be a lie if she said she did feel that way then because she still remembered moments in which she wanted desperately to fit in, moments in which she was ready to change how she was just to make friends easier.

I was happy to see Mai had stumbled upon a different culture that was more nurturing to the person she was destined to become. I was glad to see Mai had found a more understanding and inclusive culture in London to welcome every bit of her multidimensional self. Finally, I was delighted to witness the direct impact that a multicultural society had on Mai's sense of belonging in the world.

In her case, she was just raised to thrive in a culturally weird one (the UK) instead of fitting into a culturally rigid one (France).

And look at the huge difference it made!

BUBBLE BURSTING

(Forever 15)

"If you're here physically but there mentally, then where are you exactly?" Ms. S suddenly asked me during one of our weekly sessions.

This question stuck with me for what felt like an eternity.

Ms. S was my first shrink in life and I was introduced to her in my first month or so of being in boarding school. I liked her a lot because she listened to me and my problems. She never solved anything, though, which did cause a lot of frustration for me at times because while I felt better talking to her, the second I stepped outside her office, my sadness crept back within me almost immediately. She asked me interesting questions throughout the session, questions I didn't have answers to, but I found myself thinking about them on a daily basis.

I didn't know how to answer that day's question. I just knew I wasn't there mentally because this new life didn't correspond to the person I was before arriving there. I tried explaining to Ms. S. that apart from the changes in terms of activities and lifestyle—which, in my humble opinion, was already a huge change for a fifteen-year-old—a big part of my identity was lost in this new place because no one understood me fully.

And I didn't have anyone around to fully identify with.

Her question startled me a bit when she asked, "*What about the Vietnamese international students? Do you share these experiences with them?*"

I was not exactly sure how to react to this benevolent question of hers, but I knew right then that she had also just seen me as another Vietnamese international student—due to my passport and ethnicity, perhaps?—without the rest of my complex identity affiliation.

I was too tired to explain to her—or anyone, for that matter—my internal battle between my French and my Vietnamese identities. I was too exhausted to tell her I was tired of being a Vietnamese international student in an American boarding school because I wasn't sure what was expected of me with such a title. I was too worn out to tell her how dumb I felt sometimes when I was with my new Vietnamese friends in school because our laughs were not always synchronized, because I always got the jokes some seconds later, or because I just didn't understand them at all and only laughed to not feel stupid.

Looking back, I guess I felt uncomfortable there because a new identity was somehow imposed on me by my surroundings, and I wasn't exactly sure how to act or behave. I remember being cold-called on by my American History teacher in class when we were discussing the Vietnam War. He did so because he genuinely was interested in my view and perspective about this topic and most probably because he wanted to give the whole class the "other side" of the story. His intention was, indeed, kind, but little did he know, I didn't have enough knowledge of the topic to be talking about it.

I didn't feel legitimate enough to even make any comment about it.

I never studied this topic in depth when I was in the French school because it wasn't a focus in the French curriculum. We rarely spoke about the war at home because we were too busy talking about happier things, perhaps. The only person with whom I spoke about the war was my grandmother, but she never taught me historical facts and dates.

In fact, I didn't think any Vietnamese person who experienced the war would have spoken about it with facts and dates because this story was way too close and personal to be treated like a historical event.

My grandmother's narrative was more in the form of stories of how my grandfather left for China to part take in the efforts of strategizing the reconstruction of Vietnam after the war, while she stayed at home and built a bakery business to feed her community. She told me stories of how she gave out flour, breads, and cakes to Vietnamese civilians and soldiers the second she received news of the American army entering the city. She recounted the pain she felt after having distributed all she could to her people, she subsequently had to burn down all the factories and the rest of her inventories just to make sure the American soldiers weren't going to benefit from what was duly Vietnamese.

And here I was, sitting in a very American classroom in the quintessential American state of Connecticut. I wanted to laugh out loud at the irony of the scene. I was not only in what would once be deemed, by my grandmother, as the enemy's territory, but also learning their history and language and culture. I realized for such a strong and proud nation like Vietnam, I really didn't belong.

Frankly speaking, apart from my grandmother's stories, I didn't know anything about the war. I wondered whether the other Vietnamese students would have known better than I did. I thought they most probably would because they must have studied it in depth at school and from an authentic Vietnamese perspective. I didn't feel authentically Vietnamese. In fact, I never had. So when I was asked to share my opinion, in front of an American classroom, I immediately felt like an impostor. I knew I couldn't represent such a heroic nation and people because I never fully belonged to them in the first place.

I felt my face getting red and only said, "Well in Vietnam we call it the 'American War' because we never started it."

And that was probably the only thing I knew, factually, about that war.

Throughout my two years in boarding school, I thought a lot about my identity issues, firstly because I had way too much time to kill. Secondly—*and more importantly*—because I realized, for the first time, that whatever was happening inside of me was becoming problematic, for many different reasons. And I guess the most important reason was my change of status: I was no longer part of the majority of those people whose sense of belonging was often split between different nations.

Suddenly, I found myself being a part of nothing.

I stayed awake late at night wondering whether there were other people like myself in school, who just didn't know where to really put themselves. How ironic, I thought, I had to travel to the other side of the world to really grasp and understand that the Vietnam I knew and grew up in was just a very small bubble of a much bigger Vietnam. Indeed, I had always been part of the highly sheltered minority of the world. My culture shock left me with a sudden void I couldn't seem to fill.

I didn't know what to fill it with.

In fact, my Vietnam was very international where there were white people and black people and every-shade-in-between kind of people. My Vietnam was a multilingual country in which everyone spoke different languages, primarily French, English, and Vietnamese, though none of them fluently. Somehow that was never an obstacle to laughter and communication.

My Vietnam followed the Premiers League every year, with an important penchant for Manchester United, while also supporting the Vietnamese team at the Southeast Asian Games or the French team at the World Cup. My Vietnam was very free in ways that the Western world would never know, especially for young people, but also extremely authoritarian in endless approaches that I personally would never be able to grasp. My Vietnam was filled with diversity and paradoxes.

Upon arriving to my American school, I realized neither my American peers nor my Vietnamese peers had the same version of the Vietnam I once lived in.

Very quickly and painfully, I realized I was the only remnant of that world I once belonged to because everything and everyone around me had changed. My previous world turned out to be a carefully crafted bubble, one that was constructed by international school systems and parents who put their kids into them knowing that universe was not what the real world looked like. I was convinced that what parents and international school administrators were doing was building the world of the future and they were both preparing us kids to enter that next stage.

Except the future was *now* for me and I was royally fucked.

I felt like I was living in some sort of utopian dream for as long as I could remember and suddenly woke up in this new life in which I just didn't belong. I felt betrayed in many ways by the people I loved most. Despite my better judgment, I started to blame my parents a lot for the identity crisis I was going through at the time because they had previously put me in a world that was neither real nor sustainable.

They had sold me a pipe dream I now knew I would never achieve.

DONATIEN SARDIN: THE ART OF LETTING GO

———

What a surreal moment to be sitting in front of someone I once knew very well and talking about such an intimate topic—that of identity and being a weird culture kid. The last time Don and I really hung out was almost two decades ago, when we were both kids growing up in Hanoi. Now, fifteen plus years later, we were sitting face to face as late-twenties adults, acting as if we had just said our goodbyes to each other the previous week.

It hit me, almost like a surprise, he was very much alive and breathing and interacting in this weird space between us called the "virtual world." This instance transported me into the land of Yahoo and MSN messenger that we once experienced together as little children.

It felt awkwardly casual.

The interview started straight away after we exchanged some pleasantries and polite conversation. Donatien Sardin was my friend in elementary school from age six to twelve, and just like every other expat kid who lived in Vietnam transiently, his family eventually moved on to another country, this time to Cairo, Egypt, when he was twelve. As Facebook happened only in our high school years, we never really stayed in touch, perhaps only to politely wish each other a happy birthday.

Even so, it only happened intermittently.

Throughout the interview, we didn't talk much about our time in Vietnam, perhaps for fear of falling too deeply into the land of nostalgia, which wasn't the point of our call. I noticed from the beginning his reluctance to bring the past into the conversation—*the Vietnamese past, that is*—and I accepted it. So I let him talk to me about his life in Cairo instead, while allowing my wild imagination to mentally place pharaohs and other Egyptian clichés anywhere I possibly could within that six-year-span of his life.

There was a lot of affection in the way he spoke about his Egyptian experience and the friends he made there, friends who moved to France with him after their high school graduation and with whom he still remained friends today. They were a group of people like him, he claimed. People who didn't really fit into any one specific culture or country due to their privileged upbringing and their status of being expat kids.

As a weird culture kid, one of the hardest things for Donatien to come to terms with was his way of processing time. He explained to me—*methodically and almost scientifically*—how his life was broken into four different episodes with each one corresponding to a specific period of his life. The first episode was his first six years in France where he was born and lived like any other regular French kid. Then, his life took a different dimension when he arrived in Vietnam, where he would live out his boyhood in an international environment from age six to twelve. This international life and environment continued for an additional six years in Cairo, Egypt, before he returned to France at the age of eighteen and stayed ever since.

It was in this North African country where he spent his most formative years, shaping the person he was meant to become, from the age of twelve to eighteen. He talked to me about his first drinking experience or his rebellious moments when he broke into empty buildings to hang out with his friends. Apparently it was something expat kids did quite regularly in Cairo, partly because they were just being kids (the regular kind), but also partly because they simply could do whatever they wanted to do (the expat kind).

He explained to me in details the weird feeling of living in a host culture. He was never an active part of it but rather just as an audience member. They were kids who lived and grew up in a society that wasn't theirs and this awareness made them realize the local rules, customs, and expectations did not apply to them. They had their own little world of international kids who hung out together and spent time watching *MTV* and *Cartoon Network* because that was their world's norms. Anything outside of it didn't concern them, for they were not part of that bigger world just yet.

After his high school graduation, Donatien returned—*is this even the correct verb?*—to his motherland to attend university in Paris. Ever since, the French capital had taken him in, slowly but surely. Paris was where he found himself today, living out the fourth episode of his life. The way Donatien's mind processed it, he had lived three different lives prior to his current Parisian one.

I gave him a weird look, as if to show him my difference in opinion, although there was nothing to disagree with because he was just describing his own experience. He affirmed this was a subjective method he had built for himself to not only move on from the previous places he once called home, but also to encourage himself to be fully present in the new home he had consciously chosen.

"It was not just the external world because I also had to change internally and say goodbye to the person I once was in the previous places," he offered.

"Why couldn't you continue being who you were?" I asked him while wondering internally whether this statement meant I was, in fact, just interviewing a total stranger over Google Meet.

"For me, continuity only made sense if I was not the only remaining element of the life I once lived. But unfortunately, I was. So I needed to change. I needed to adapt and to fit in," he asserted.

How brutal life could be for supposedly the most privileged kids, I thought to myself. I paused for a while to gather my thoughts. I felt grateful for his willingness to share these intimate experiences, many of which I could already mirror in my own growing up process. He helped me out before words came back to me.

"That was why I didn't get in touch with people in my past lives; I needed to let go fully to move on and be happy again," Donatien admitted.

Was that his way of apologizing for never getting in touch with his friends from Vietnam?

Suddenly, I caught myself being very envious of his ability to have his several lives nicely packed into different boxes. I imagined different colored shelves where these boxes sat neatly, one next to the other, each with its own carefully written label. Each with its own specific tag and time period.

I imagined each of these boxes corresponded with a step of his journey—*his different lives, as he called them*—that had brought him all the way to this exact moment where he was now sitting in front of his computer and speaking to someone who belonged to one of the first boxes of his life. I imagined it must have felt, for him, like he was just going through an old photo album in his parents' attic on a rainy Saturday afternoon. Except this photo was more recent and it wasn't static.

It felt awkwardly comfortable.

I paused my imagination and came back to my rational mind. I wanted to disagree with him completely about his time-processing technique and compartmentalization process. I wanted to throw at him accusatory questions like "How can you be whole, when you've let go of everything that came before that?" or "Where do you even start to humanly or emotionally compartmentalize these years into boxes?"

And most importantly, "Where exactly did you bury them?"

Of course, I didn't verbalize any of those questions and managed to snap out of my internal mindset almost immediately. I noticed I was actually really envious of where he was right now—a place of complete acceptance I had yet to discover. I felt hopeful because he had shown me what it could potentially look like from the other side of wherever I was, internally. He confessed that his method, coupled with time (what felt like an eternity of time), had worked rather well for him. If only it could be a generic formula, I thought, because from my view, he looked genuinely whole and happy.

And who didn't want to be whole and happy?

I smiled while not really knowing how to feel about his decade-long silence. He continued explaining that the interesting and maybe most special element of his compart-mentalization strategy was his ability to remember many details of every single one of his previous lives. Even though I initially found his statement to be conflictive—*how can you let go completely while still having vivid memories?*—I admitted this to be true because he had previously spoken about memories I had completely forgotten about. Memories we shared together that my mind had reduced to mere moments while taking its magical flair away and deprived them of their rightful status as memories.

As a very forgetful person, I wondered whether, contrary to Donatien, I had chosen to forget as my own way to cope with change while growing up as a weird culture kid.

As I rewatched our interview for the umpteenth time to write this chapter, something within me finally clicked. Donatien had taught me a very important lesson through his observation that day. He showed me the difference between letting go (what he had gloriously achieved) and forgetting (what I erroneously tricked myself into achieving).

In fact, letting go was never about forgetting but about the ability to stop carrying one's past experiences into one's present ones. Letting go was never about forgetting but about a person's courage to stop constantly comparing the present moment with their previous ones. Letting go was never about forgetting but about surrendering to the present moment and accepting it wholeheartedly.

He was still the same person I used to know, I realized. His essence, I felt, was still there. He was no longer just a French student living in a foreign country and enrolled in an international school system because his reality had changed. And that didn't make him any less of a weird culture kid than he once was.

We quickly wrapped up our interview session and said our goodbyes. Almost like magic, I clicked the red button to end the call. As I released him back into his current life, I wished him a lifetime—*and all the future lives that he may live*—of happiness.

MENTAL LIVING

———

(Finally 16)

For the first time in my life, I felt like both my French and Vietnamese conflicting identities were slipping away from me, leaving me with absolutely nothing to hold on to. My new American environment exacerbated my identity issues not only because it further highlighted the differences between my way of being Vietnamese and the more traditional way of being Vietnamese, but also because it completely took my French identity away from me.

On the one hand, I felt like I was losing that innate authority and legitimacy of being Vietnamese in this foreign land because my version of it didn't correspond to that of most of the Vietnamese students around me. On the other hand, no one considered me French because no one around me could either confirm or acknowledge that part of my identity. I couldn't blame them because honestly, how could they have known? Nothing about my way of being could have given them some clues about my affiliation. Not in the food

I ate, which was American cafeteria food. Not in the way I spoke because I never mentioned anything French for fear of appearing odd or even snobby. Not even in my appearance because I simply looked Vietnamese.

For a long time, I kept to myself because I didn't know who I was supposed to be anymore. Since I didn't know who I was, I couldn't make real friends because I didn't know who to gravitate toward or who to approach. I often felt like I was just existing in this new world while my real self was somewhere living a much happier life, filled with people who understood her truest self, her inner self. Many times, I caught myself dreaming of this distant and almost foreign life I wasn't living, which wasn't entirely mine to claim. Then I came back to reality and buried myself in school work to kill time.

I picked up tons of different extracurricular activities to kill some more time. I took private singing and piano lessons every week—*activities I had never signed up for willingly prior to Connecticut.* I joined a softball team while thinking to myself every day I was going to get a concussion because I had never been very athletic. I signed up for volunteer work to go spend time with older people or tutor underprivileged kids.

I wanted to make myself feel better and being busy seemed, at the time, like the best way to do so.

Until today, I still think of those two years in boarding school as the hardest years of my life. I think I was so badly damaged because I had lost everything I had always built my identity on or around. I had lost a city and a country. I had lost all the people who knew me and, as a consequence, all of the previous versions of myself. I had lost my old lifestyle and rhythm of life. I had even lost my sense of self.

It felt, at times, that I really didn't have anything else to lose.

Needless to say, I lived mostly in my head—*in a constant state of denial*—because I couldn't find anyone to identify with. I found it very difficult to forge strong relationships with those around me. I continued crying myself to sleep almost every night. Once or twice, I woke up in the middle of the night for no reason and just cried. On one particular occasion, it got really intense. I fell asleep quite early and for some reason woke up in the middle of the night. I didn't know what to do with myself and a rather odd thought came into my head.

At that point in time, I was participating in this program where I would go to this kids' center and hang out and tutor them once a week after school. A teacher would drive us in a van to get to that center and we would make a quick stop on the way back to school at Dunkin' Donuts for a treat. Most of the time I would buy a lot of donuts and share with people or just keep them in my room as if they were gold. And that would, more often than not, be the highlight of my week.

When this thought came into my mind, a very strong sense of self-pity surged within me. How pathetic, I thought, that this had become the highlight of my week. What had become of my life? How did things change so fast? Why was I so miserable? And just like that, the questioning spiral would go on for quite some time before, out of exhaustion, I could fall asleep.

I often counted the days until I could return to Vietnam for vacations. As a kid who used to love school and hated summer holidays, I transformed into this kid who loved vacations—*all sorts of vacations*—and built countdown timers until the day I would go back to Hanoi to pick up that girl I left behind.

I did feel blessed to be able to fly home three times a year, a privilege I never took for granted. I remember after the first time I came home for Christmas during my first year abroad, I returned to boarding school at the end of the break and never unpacked my suitcase. I detested my new life so much that I would literally live out of a suitcase to trick myself into thinking this was only temporary.

My denial was going strong.

At around the same time, I developed a habit of speaking to my old friends in my head. This was because they were too busy having fun to answer me on Facebook. I was never angry at them, ever, because before attending boarding school, I never would have thought this was how the outside world looked and felt like. I was very reluctant to share everything with my friends at home because I didn't want to be the party pooper. I didn't want to tell them they were living in a bubble—*and not a world*—and everything was going to change the second they graduated from high school and closed the Vietnam chapter to open a new one elsewhere.

My habit of speaking with my old friends went even further at times. For instance, sometimes when I was speaking to my new schoolmates in the cafeteria or other social areas, I would be simultaneously having a different conversation with my friends in Vietnam in my head. It was almost like an out-of-body experience, commenting on the conversation I was having in real life, as if I wasn't actively taking part in that moment but was just a spectator of it.

I knew internally this double life I was living was extremely unhealthy, but at the same time, it was the thing that comforted me most.

As if that wasn't enough—*because it clearly wasn't*—I cultivated a rather strange habit I still keep today: the habit of dancing alone in my room with the lights off while blasting music on my iPod (because iPod was still a thing at that moment).

It was a daily evening activity, one that mirrored my Hanoian nightlife. Every night, after lights out, either before or after crying (because some crying was always involved), I danced. It was always a very ceremonious moment because in my head, I was still dancing in Hanoi.

Most—*if not all*—of the time, tears would come to me in these daily dancing sessions because of one of these two scenarios. Either I let my mind wander on Facebook that evening and got intensely FOMOed (it wasn't yet a thing back then) and started crying and, almost as if to self-medicate, I dressed up and pretended I, too, was in those pictures and was dancing with them all night long.

Or, I would be in a really good mood that evening and wanted to dance to express this optimism. As I came out of my trance and fantasy to change into my pajamas and crawl into bed, my real Connecticut life would hit me straight in the face. Crying usually exhausted me enough for me to be able to fall asleep.

Oftentimes, it was easier to be in the first scenario because by the end of it, I always felt slightly better.

The most embarrassing moment of my boarding school life happened during sophomore year. My day was going well when I came back to my room from lunch and decided I was going to dance to kill time. I was feeling particularly happy on that day. It was a celebration dance rather than an antidepressant one. The time was 2:00 p.m. The song was *Womanizer* by Britney Spears. The volume was 100 percent. The costume was a very nice and flowery dress from Zara.

During the first minute of the song, I felt ecstatic and happy and joyful. I had trained my brain to be happy on command but on that particular day, I felt genuinely happy. I felt a tiny bit more myself. When the chorus arrived and Britney's voice went all the way up to sing the chorus, I decided to jump up in the air.

The next second, I was on the ground, screaming due to a very acute pain in my right ankle.

Because the music was so loud on my iPod, I hadn't realized I had screamed at the top of my lungs upon landing on that cold, cold floor. Seconds later, a girl whom I had been friendly with ran into my room and saw me on the floor. She immediately rushed toward me to collect my weeping self and helped me sit on my bed. Once I had collected myself, she went to get the nurse to come and help me with my sprained ankle while I changed out of my ridiculous Thursday, 2-ish outfit.

Buddha bless her, that dormmate never mentioned that incident to anyone else.

Myself included.

LLAMAS TRIBE

(Age 16)

A very weird girl came into my life with a mouth guard a couple months after my arrival at boarding school.

I didn't know what a mouth guard was, so my eyes followed her every move in the kitchen. She expertly boiled water in a casserole, popped her mouth guard in it, and patiently waited. We were having regular small talk before it happened:

She put the mouth guard into her mouth to mold it while I burst out in uncontrollable laughter. I had never seen anything similar before. Not even at the dentist.

Her name was Nicole and she was my dormmate. That was how little I paid attention to the world around me; I didn't even know we were living in the same two-story house.

I don't recall the details of how exactly we became friends, but I remember Nicole telling me she was Korean but her family was in Seattle.

"So you're Korean-American?" I asked.

"No, I'm Korean, but my family lives in Seattle for now," she calmly explained.

She, too, was a "for now" kid.

Upon learning this fact, I decided Nicole was my kind of person because her story was very similar to those of my French friends in Vietnam. I found myself liking her immediately. Maybe because I found myself having very quirky conversations with her. Maybe because she was just culturally as weird as I was, although she seemed to have a very black and white view of her identity—*unlike myself.*

She would tell everyone she was Korean but her family was temporarily living in Seattle, a detail that was crucial to Nicole's introduction of herself. The detail I would have added to mine would be I attended a French international school my whole life.

But I never did.

Nicole was one of the first people in school that I felt like I could identify and build a strong relationship with. I wanted to know why her name was Nicole and not something more similar to the names of the other Korean kids. I wanted to know why she was friendly with me instead of the many other Koreans who were also in school with us.

With time, I noticed she didn't have many Korean friends and as we grew closer, I observed some small elements that set her apart from the other Korean kids in school.

The most noticeable feature was that she didn't bow to the older Korean students—like most Koreans did between one another—but simply waved at them whenever she saw them while simultaneously saying "Annyeonghaseyo," which meant "hi" in Korean. I mentioned my observation to her once and she looked very surprised that I even noticed.

"It's such a Korean thing to bow your head when seeing older people because the society is so hierarchical," she complained.

"So why don't you do it?" I curiously asked.

"I just don't see the purpose of it. And besides, we're in America now," she answered plainly.

"Would you have done it in Korea?" I pressed.

She looked at me amused, most probably because no one had ever asked her that question before.

"I used to when I was younger. Now I would think twice before I did it. Otherwise, I would need to be in a specific situation to do so," she replied.

Not long after our first encounter, Nicole introduced me to two other girls, Jahee and Audrey, whom I met over dinner at Arugula, our soon-to-be favorite restaurant in Hartford, Connecticut.

Just like Nicole, Jahee was a Korean living in America, though she had always kept her Korean name because it was easy enough for Americans to pronounce. Jahee was more like myself, I thought, because her parents still lived in Korea and her siblings were also attending boarding school and university in the States. But unlike me, Jahee was sent to the States from the age of eight.

Weirdly enough her sense of home was still very much tied to Korea.

"How come?" I blurted out.

"Because I still go back there regularly and that's where my parents are based," she answered matter-of-factly.

Jahee went on to explain to me that her two siblings also went through the same journey from a very young age and that made her feel less lost and destabilized. She knew there were at least two other people who knew exactly what she went through. And the mere knowledge of their existence gave her a strong sense of normalcy.

Meeting Jahee made me question my sense of "home" more frequently. I found it odd that Jahee still found a sense of home in her parents, despite the time and distance that separated them. Was the feeling of belonging to a family innate, regardless of the time spent together? Was belonging not measured in the amount of memories or the volume of laughter?

And how can Jahee still feel Korean despite living in the United States for 80 percent of her life? Wasn't she American-Korean by now?

"Of course I'm not American-Korean; I don't have the same problems as the Korean immigrants to the US. I'm just here for school and school happens to be very long," she patiently explained.

As I got to know her better, I realized Jahee and I shared many commonalities. Jahee didn't speak fluently either Korean or English, but was somehow fluent in the combination of these two languages. I knew of her lack of fluency in English because I was her designated writer throughout high school, not necessarily because I wanted to help her, but because I wanted her to graduate. As to her Korean deficiency, it was confirmed by Nicole's frequent facial expressions in their Korean exchanges, which usually ended with Nicole asking Jahee to switch to English.

I could so relate.

"I eat American, speak American, and wear American. At the same time, I also exaggerate my bows when I cross paths with Korean people and my sense of responsibilities toward my family is extremely heightened. I think this happens because subconsciously I want to balance out my American side with my Korean one," she explained to me after taking a moment to think about her identity.

"I guess I am just a very Americanized Korean," Jahee concluded and remained, until today, one of my most intriguing case studies.

Audrey was named after Audrey Hepburn—her mother's favorite artist—and to a certain extent, she did remind me of the actual actress. My Audrey was tall, beautiful, and Chinese with a very high-pitched voice. In my initial perception, Audrey was a very Westernized Asian because my definition of being Asian was solely based on Vietnamese people.

"Audrey is my birth name," she once told me as I mistakenly thought that, like Nicole who chose a Western name in school, Audrey did, too. She taught me that it was very common for Hong-Kongese to have Western names and to speak English.

"I grew up with both afternoon tea time and dim sum Sundays," she would mention in one of our endless conversations. And that simple comment gave me a much clearer view of what Hong Kong was as a society and who Audrey was as a person.

Audrey and I were similar in that we both went to international schools, though I went to a French one in Vietnam, and she went to an American one in Hong Kong. And this mere difference had turned Audrey, from day one, into my intellectual challenger. I learned a lot from her in our exchanges about the different international school systems that we had previously experienced before landing in boarding school. Naturally, Audrey was always defending her American school system because it happened to be one that she fervently believed in, one that had been so strongly anchored in herself.

She philosophized about the importance of attending classes that corresponded to your intellectual level and not solely based on your age. She stressed the fundamental need to meet new people in different classes because that was crucial for the development of one's open-mindedness toward the world. She emphasized the necessity of choosing one's own classes to take responsibility for oneself and one's actions.

It took me quite some time to not only intellectually grasp these new concepts, but also to come to an agreement with some of them, and I credit Audrey for that. My French defiance, naturally, came out during these conversations that I often turned into debates, simply because that was how I was taught to develop a critical mind in the French system.

The four of us formed an atypical clique, one made up of those who didn't necessarily want to fully adopt the culture of the host country because our loyalty and affiliation lay in another culture—or several ones—but, at the same time, we found it very difficult to leave the host country because now that our cultural identity was so diluted, maybe moving back to our official motherland didn't make sense any more.

Meeting these women-to-be made me feel much less lonely because I registered, for the first time, that there were many people out there in my new world who were also going through the same identity-questioning process as myself. I realized I was, after all, not that special.

And this realization made me feel surprisingly lighter and happier.

Slowly and seamlessly, they became my new reference system. Thanks to their own identity confusion, they understood me sometimes better than I understood myself. They saw beyond my nationality, which also included the less seen aspects of my cultural heritage. They asked me for French music and movie suggestions while simultaneously requesting phở recipes and fish sauce brands.

They didn't expect anything of me that I wasn't already.

Having discussions with these girls was also the first time in my life that I had even tried to put words on these different identities and feelings. They offered me a space to analyze and better understand my weird aspects, for they too, were very weird in this new norm that we were introduced into.

Collectively.

PEACEMAKING

(Age 16 and Beyond)

I noticed that since my arrival in the United States, as I had lost all of my previous reference points, I was given a new canvas to play with and explore my cultural identity. I developed an internal system where I would be measuring myself on a scale of total cultural belonging on one side to total cultural estrangement on the other. While living in Vietnam, I would have two different scales at all times, the French one and the Vietnamese one, on which I vacillated often as I jumped from my role as a student at the international French school during the day to that of a member of a Vietnamese household in the evening.

But the scales, I believed, would never go to the extreme for either one of the cultures when they were averaged together. In fact, it would always remain somewhere in the middle with perhaps a slight inclination toward total cultural belonging to the French society because of not only my education at school, but also of my social life and of the

Western entertainment industry of which I was exposed to 24/7.

Now that I was living in the United States, I was most probably estranged from the French culture because the only things around me that were deemed "French" were toasts and fries. Not to mention that no one recognized the French part of my identity, apart from Madame. The few times when I might have muttered the courage to tell people around me that I spoke fluent French, I was waiting for them to ask me more interesting questions so I could have a chance to fully develop my narrative.

But most of the time, I would get some comments along the lines of "Oh yes, of course you speak French because Vietnam was a colony of France." I was sure the person with whom I was speaking to must have felt extremely proud and worldly for such a response. "Yes, Vietnam was a colony of France, but no, that wasn't why I spoke French," I wanted to answer. But instead, I remained quiet. In retrospect, I wonder whether the reason behind my profound sadness was my grieving of that unseen French-ness within me.

Simultaneously, I noticed that my belonging to the Vietnamese culture grew, exponentially, while living abroad. I believed it was mainly because of the new identity that was somewhat erroneously put on me. Overnight, boarding school placed this new cloak on me that turned me into the walking and breathing representation of Vietnam in Connecticut.

And that made me question a lot of things about myself and my previous life.

It made me question the definition of being Vietnamese—in my own terms. Quite ironically, I had learned a lot about Vietnam, my motherland, only since moving to the United States. Perhaps it was exactly because I was carrying the responsibility of representing such a nation without any previous real or deep connection to the country that made the nerd in me dig up endless articles about the history of Vietnam and engage in interview-like conversations with my new Vietnamese friends just to better understand the country, the culture, and its people.

It felt oddly familiar when I was hanging out with my Vietnamese friends at school because I was vacillating between the "us" and the "them." My new friends reminded me a lot of my cousins whom I was awfully close with back in Vietnam but at the same time very different from in hundreds of ways.

With them, too, I noticed how I was able to pick and choose when I identified myself as a Vietnamese and when I didn't.

I noted those things religiously to give myself a sense of control of who I was inwardly. And with time, I felt myself fully accepted, not necessarily as a "Vietnamese-Vietnamese," but as a Vietnamese of a different kind. A subcategory of Vietnamese. This made me think of a very widespread saying in Southeast Asian countries—mainly Vietnam, Thailand, Laos, and Cambodia—"same-same but different."

If you know, you know.

With retrospect, I grew to be forgiving of my experience in boarding school, while acknowledging the constant emptiness and misery I carried within me every single day throughout those two years. I now thought differently of that period of my life. I used to blame the external factors for all the negative emotions I felt while attending that school.

I now know that although external factors such as the rules, the discipline, and the rural environment did indeed play a very important role in harboring my sorrow, the extreme pain I was enduring was rather heavily due to the identity crisis I was going through, caused by a sense of total loss and not belonging.

Today, twelve years later, I finally understand that loss always came hand in hand with change, while not belonging was an automatic state of any uprooted weird culture kid.

I came to realize my original home was the international school environment for that was the world in which I grew up and spent most of my formative years. That was the world I believed to be truest to my sense of self until today. It was only in that world where I found myself normal and belonging to a very diverse majority. A majority that ate all sorts of food at home and spoke many different languages at school. A majority that was constantly negotiating their identity in terms of a group but also on an individual case by case basis.

I still believed in that world—*even though I had come to realize it was more of a bubble*—and reminisced about it often. Maybe—*just maybe*—if the international school system was more accessible to everyone else, in the long run, I would stop thinking of myself as a "weird culture kid," for I would then belong to the majority of the world and not to the minority like I did now.

Maybe—*just maybe*—if I followed in my parents footsteps and also bet on the future of the international school system like they once did, and if enough people also took that bet, then one day, not too far away, that global and international world would not only be transposed into the real world, but would also completely become the real world, for the gap that separated the local and global universes would sharpen and eventually collide.

Only then would the culture shock endured by so many of today's "weird culture kids" diminish. Only then would our world stop being a bubble. Only then would our norms become more normal.

MARCO GARCIA: PERMANENTLY IMPERMANENT

—

I timidly wrote to Marco Garcia, my classmate at the French school in Hanoi from the age of seven to twelve, to ask him to grant me an interview for my book. And to my biggest surprise, he said "yes."

Even though I have been carrying out these conversations with all sorts of people—*friends, acquaintances, strangers*—I wasn't quite sure where to place Marco. I wasn't sure whether he was an acquaintance or a stranger by now, given the enormous lapse of time that had inserted itself between our life then and our life now.

The minute he connected and said "hello," my worries disappeared. He had a voice I didn't recognize or remember hearing before, but oddly enough, it was a voice filled with a sense of warmth and genuineness. And just like that, we dived right into a fascinating interview in which he shared with me his specific relationship with time—*or the ephemeral aspect of it.*

Marco's father was French and his mother Peruvian, but unlike other mixed kids who spoke two different languages at home, one with each parent, Marco wasn't brought up that way. His mother tongue was Spanish, and it was the language used in his household from as long as he could remember, whether through the lullabies he listened to as a toddler or the Disney animation movies he watched as a kid.

French was only introduced when he started attending school as he was growing up. So with time, Marco also became fluent in French, his father tongue.

Like all of my previous interviews, I asked Marco where he was from.

He answered confidently that he was of French and Peruvian cultures but grew up in the French schools around the world. From the moment he was born until the age of eighteen, Marco was living with his family abroad. He was born in Lima, Peru, but soon moved to Mexico City because of his father's job.

After his toddler years, he left the North American continent to move to Asia. It was in the French school in Hanoi where we met and remained classmates for five years. After Hanoi, he went to France for a year before leaving again, this time to Milan, Italy, for three years.

His senior year in high school was spent in France where, for the first time, he truly realized he was different from the other kids around him. Unlike his previous relocations, this time Marco no longer found himself in the international world of the French lycées abroad. He no longer sat in the same classrooms as other expat kids, all coming from many different countries and cultures in the world.

This time, kids like him were no longer the norm but the minority.

This was his first major experience of integrating in the French culture, a culture that was supposed to be innately his.

Marco remembers taking a longer period of time to adapt to France and to his new school, specifically. In terms of size, it was much bigger than the international French schools he was used to when living abroad. In fact, this new school seemed like a maze to him. The building itself was much bigger, the student body much more numerous, though never as diverse.

Marco came from a small expat world where everybody knew everybody to a huge local one where no one seemed to know anyone.

Up to this point, the French education system abroad had been one of the main constants in Marco's life, as if it was a third parent who watched over him as he grew into the person he wanted to be.

Upon his return to the motherland for his senior year in high school, Marco realized his reference point for all of these years was extremely helpful in some ways, but not all ways. In fact, it was a place where he was taught French history and French literature, but not the reality of living in the French society or the mentality of French people. He remembers how much harder it was for him to feel some sense of belonging in his new French lycée.

Despite his rather difficult reintegration into French society, he succeeded and ended up staying in France for almost a decade now. Marco admitted to not thinking about his childhood often but now that he was actively doing it with someone else, he felt a somewhat familiar sense of longing for the past that he hadn't felt in a long time. We wondered together whether it was because we were carefree children our memories were as sweet and loving as we remember them today, or if our past was truly that exceptional, which made it much harder for us to detach ourselves from it.

Probably a bit of both.

Marco admitted that whenever he thought of Hanoi—*which was less and less*—he pictured the concrete courtyard where we used to run around despite the excruciating heat that seemed to be the only season in Hanoi. I felt a lot of joy simply because we talked about things I no longer thought of. Things we once loved. People we once knew on varying levels. Marco observed that ever since leaving Vietnam, he had never been in such a diverse classroom. We talked about our Korean, Australian, and Italian classmates. We pronounced names we hadn't said in many, many years.

It felt like we were visiting an entirely different life.

"Are you going to have an expat life?" I asked Marco, as if we were children again, dreaming about the different "when I grow up" scenarios.

"I was expecting your question to be 'do you miss your life abroad?'" he joked over the phone. And like the smart cookie I remembered him to be, his answer was twofold: (1) yes, he missed traveling but (2) no, he didn't miss the expat life.

What a typical answer for a WCK—always seeing things from different angles while never going for the easy option. The tone of the conversation suddenly shifted. I could feel the authenticity in his voice, which instinctively revealed the fact that he must have pondered this question hundreds, if not thousands, of times before.

"I believe that children need some form of continuity in their life, especially when they are growing up. And I would want my children to have that."

"Did you wish to not grow up as an expat kid?" I asked him timidly, almost afraid to hear what he had to say.

"No, I don't wish that because those are the best years of my life. I just wished I could have stayed longer because five years in a place, especially one that you loved so much, didn't seem enough."

Is any amount of time ever enough to live in a moment that you so thoroughly enjoyed?

We discussed at length Marco's desire to extend time at a place and the sense of discontinuity he felt while growing up. He described to me the perceived difficulty he attached to the act of building something—anything—meaningful because he knew he was leaving some years later. As if everything in his life—*from his morning routines to his friendships*—had an expiration date. I imagined how unfinished his every adventure must have felt every single time. The forced endings and lack of closure must have triggered and developed the importance he put on continuity in his life today.

Most definitely because of his experiences growing up, the person Marco was today had forged a rather firm belief that everything with value must be given time. In his exact words, *"Value is the prize that you get because you have invested a lot of your time in it—whatever 'it' is."*

I sincerely hope he didn't think his childhood was of no value.

I wanted to tell him that five years was actually a very considerable amount of time. Without them, we would never have this conversation today. Without them, he would not have many memories to carry with him. Without them, he wouldn't have many things to miss. After all, how much time is enough time to say goodbye? To love a person? To forget a place?

What if we overspent our time on something and spoiled it instead of leaving it while it was still at its best?

Before I could attack him with all of my unanswered questions, he shared what sounded almost like a secret. He told me that when he was growing up, every summer, regardless of where he was in the world, he would always come back to France to visit his grandparents who lived in a small village at Bagnères de Luchon. This place, it turned out, was extremely important for Marco because it was the only place that remained stable throughout his formative years.

"The benefit of living in a village," he further explained, "is that everything stayed the same: same roads, same mountains, same people at the tennis club."

He affirmed that this place, ultimately, was so important because it gave him a very pleasant impression of permanence.

And forever an impression it will remain.

Shortly after, our time was up.

I hung up feeling like I just dialed the past and asked to speak with Marco Garcia—a person I hadn't thought of in many, many years.

I'm glad we got to speak that day. He sure sounded like someone I'd like to know.

Again.

PART THREE

(BECAUSE I BELIEVE IN TRILOGIES)

WHO AM I?

COMING TOGETHER

———

(a Decade Later or Age 27)

My own way to cope with alienation was to journal. Writing helped a lot. Since a young age, whenever I felt confused about something, I wrote until I was no longer disoriented. I would sit down—*on my desk, on my bed, on the sofa*—and put words to paper, scratching some out along the way while adding new ones as I edited. Writing my thoughts down helped me make them more concrete, more tangible.

I relished the feeling of holding my thoughts in my hand because it gave me a sense of control over the inexplicably strange feelings I had within me. The feeling of not knowing which world to fully belong to and which country to wholly identify with.

Today, when I read through my diary entries, I have an overview of my "becoming" journey. I laugh at my rebelliousness in the French entries and my otherness in the Vietnamese ones. I noticed that whatever I lacked in identity, I added in personality. On days when I felt non-French, I would use a lot of exclamation marks—*too many exclamation marks*—in an attempt to be more assertive, a characteristic I deemed to be quintessentially French.

Similarly, whenever I wrote about my feeling of being left out during my playdates with my cousins, I noticed the Vietnamese diary entries would be shorter, almost self-effacing. Almost too shy to appear on the page. And that was mainly due to my weak Vietnamese vocabulary.

Unsurprisingly, ever since boarding school, each and every single journal entry of mine had been written in the English language—though always with a dramatic French touch and a Vietnamese downplaying flair. And these entries continued and remained in English until today. Looking back, I am extremely grateful to have given the United States a second chance after my painful boarding school experience. I'm glad I decided to stay for university and lived a completely different American experience, one that strongly forged the person I am today.

Life would never be as good without its ironic twists. Much to my French teachers' disappointment and my Vietnamese parents' annoyance, I am writing my first book in English. After all, I did graduate from an American high school and university. After all, I did live my most youthful and magical years on American soil. After all, I did find myself deeply and profoundly while living my American life.

And as a natural result of time, experience, and introspection, I've come to identify more with the American way of being than with either the French or the Vietnamese one.

I find that the American identity was much more accepting of the multicultural being I am today. It doesn't ask me to choose between France or Vietnam; instead, it allows me to be a little bit of both and then some. It doesn't ask me to fully assimilate like the French culture does, nor does it impose homogeneity onto me like the Vietnamese one. It allows me to be myself amidst the internal chaotic world I still harbor within me every day. It celebrates differences while giving me a physical place to belong.

Ultimately, the American identity has allowed me to glue together both my French and Vietnamese facets while acting as the bridge between both cultures.

So here I am, attempting to describe the duality between the French and the Vietnamese parts of my weird culture self in English prose, feeling like a breathing cliché. Perhaps it is because this third language does not carry the multitude of emotions and the history that both French and Vietnamese did for me. I find the English language to be more forgiving—of my grammar mistakes, of my pronunciation errors, of my listening inaccuracies. Perhaps because I find English to be more neutral toward me and me toward it, English has therefore allowed me to be more objective toward the stories and experiences that I am trying to convey.

Or perhaps—*just perhaps*—it was precisely thanks to my painful immersion in the American culture and language that has allowed me to develop an analytical understanding of my previous relationships with both my French and Vietnamese identities. It took a new world for me to better understand my previous one, especially when my earlier world was presented to me from such a young age and with such certainty.

As I trace back my identity journey, I cannot help but think that world politics has got a lot to do with it.

After all, I did major in government in college.

My grandparents grew up in a very different period. In fact, although they lived through the French colonial era, they didn't seem to harbor any anger or resentment toward that country. On the contrary, they seemed to be very proud of their knowledge of the French language and culture. I vividly remember the way *bà ngoai*[21] enjoyed her café au lait and Vietnamese baguette every morning for breakfast. I remember my ông nôi[22] proudly rode his Peugeot bicycle every time he came to visit my brother and me.

And every single time, without fail, he would tell us Peugeot was a French brand.

I then think about my Cold War parents who studied and worked in Moscow for many years. I think about the world in which they grew up, a world defined by the rigid dichotomy between the Eastern Bloc and the Western one, between Communism and Capitalism, between us and them.

Yet, upon our return to Vietnam from Russia, they immediately enrolled Phan and me into the French school because of the seemingly superior education that we would get.

Doesn't their entrusting of their future into the French, then American, educational systems seem like the most beautiful call for truce?

And from that decision, our normalcy was carefully crafted daily. This normalcy vacillated between the Vietnamese world at home and the French one at school. Not to mention the omnipresent American entertainment world that was embedded in both spheres from my young age until today.

No one seemed to wonder what would become of these weird culture kids.

Although I had always noticed the countless differences between my parents and me, I had also detected that ever since my leaving home for boarding school, our differences

---

21 "Maternal grandmother" in Vietnamese
22 "Paternal grandfather" in Vietnamese

had exacerbated achingly. As if our disagreements changed according to the miles that physically separated us. Slowly, all the Muscovite tales I used to hear as bedtime stories and all of the memories captured in pictures of me hanging on Dad's shoulder or Mom's arms in front of countless Russian monuments had dissipated, leaving a rather bitter aftertaste in my memory.

Throughout university, I was living in the States and was fully adhering to all the American values and principles, from diversity to equality, from unity to individualism, from liberty to self-government. I rejected my parents' support of President Putin while they never accepted my reverence for President Obama. Never in my wildest dream did I think my parents and I would clash so violently and fervently on symbols that we both held so dear to our hearts.

Were we entering some sort of Cold War due to our cultural differences?

Some years later, when President Trump got elected, I received a phone call from Dad. One that I was half expecting but too shocked to fully see it coming. It was an ordinary call when we would catch up about the most mundane stories and the most important piece of news on TV. Then Dad just adeptly inserted into our conversation before hanging up, "Look at the Free World's POTUS," he mused, "I guess America is not too different from Russia after all."

Hearing his sarcastic comment made me feel, perhaps erroneously, somewhat closer to him.

THOMAS DE RUTY: "NOW" IS YOUR BIGGEST INVESTMENT

———

From the comfort of my bedroom, I turned on the computer and found Thomas, my most consistent guy friend since the 1990s, sitting in his living room. Behind him, a wall of sculptures of (Western) Buddha's faces were staring at me. I smiled because the sight of these decorations always brought me straight home to my world in Hanoi. A world where very different cultures and elements were mixed together, where people were either Westernized Asians or Asianized Westerners, without any one specific identity—but somehow everything seemed to blend together nicely.

Thomas and I grew up together in Hanoi and even though we barely spoke these days— *yes, like many adults, we let life get in the way of our friendship*—whenever we did speak, our conversations always felt very effortless. At this point, he felt more like a brother to me, in both the best and the worst ways.

Today was a good day because I was interviewing Thomas about my favorite time and topic in life: our most amazing childhood in Vietnam. Even though I mostly wanted to know what it felt like to be a white boy living and growing up in the Vietnamese society in the 1990s and early 2000s, what Thomas shared with me was manifold. He not only taught me a lot about what it meant to be an Asianized Western-er—*a theme that I never really thought about growing up because I never had to*—he also shared with me his most brilliant insight about happiness being more than a choice, but a daily investment.

Thomas was a white halfie, son of a French dad and an Anglo-Saxon mom (*she was also definitely a weird culture kid*). From the age of three, he grew up in his big expat home in Vietnam with all the luxuries one could dream of as a kid (and also as a grown up). He often threw crazy parties in his Xuan Dieu home with a swimming pool on the rooftop from as far as I could remember and only stopped because he moved away from Hanoi at the age of eighteen. Simultaneously, he also hosted chilling sessions in his AC-ed bedroom (indeed, a very important detail for all kids who grew up in Vietnam) where we would just sit on his bed and talk for hours on end about the most fascinating things that went on in our teenage lives.

Thomas shared with me his culture at home where he spoke to his dad in French and answered his mum in English—a phenomenon I had witnessed time and time again whenever I was at his house. We discussed his confusion, at times, when he heard the Vietnamese language being spoken everywhere around him except in his household. He explained to me the different stages of his relationship to the Vietnamese language: first as a foreigner hearing unusual sounds at a very young age, then as a half-foreigner who unconsciously understood it, and eventually as a semi-local who spoke it conversationally by the end of his fifteen years as a Vietnamese resident.

Thank Buddha, I told myself quietly.

We spoke about the different cultural holidays he celebrated at home. Even the different types of food he was taught to embrace: exquisite wine and cheese, which clearly represented his French side, and casual but delicious meat pies, which represented his Anglo-Saxon one.

"I never felt weird while living in Hanoi because I had a lot of friends around me who were exactly like myself. There were a lot of halfies who also lived in Vietnam due to their parents' job," Thomas asserted.

With time, this foreign culture slowly became the one where he would strongly attach his sense of identity, while the ones he inherited by birth slowly took a secondary position. How can anyone blame him, really, because he did indeed live in Vietnam for most of his life.

Although he didn't live with the locals, he lived among the locals and slowly, inevitably, became local in his own way.

We resumed our conversation about Thomas's life as an expat boy growing up in Vietnam, an experience he summarized simply as "lacking nothing." I would even argue that we were extremely privileged—so privileged that upon leaving our parents' roof in Vietnam, we both experienced culture shock going into what was deemed the real world. Even though we both left Vietnam at very different times and went to very different places, our experiences were quite similar. Our standards of living dropped dangerously fast and all the perks we once took for granted were no longer part of our daily lives.

We no longer lived in big houses but in rather small apartments (*or shoeboxes, as I called them*). We could no longer afford to go out every day for a drink or a bite. Even the ability of taking

a *xe-ôm* ("motorbike taxi") was taken away from us and the prices of Ubers in Europe made you think twice before ordering one.

We then talked at length about the insane degree of freedom we experienced as kids—perhaps even more freedom than we could possibly handle at that age. Perhaps more freedom than we would ever be given again in life.

"Life could not have been better for young people," Thomas reminisced.

I nodded in agreement before asking him, "What did it feel like to grow up as a Westerner in Hanoi specifically?"

There was a brief pause before he proceeded with utmost honesty:

"A lot of perks and privileges were given to me simply because I was a white boy living in Vietnam. People—*real locals, that is*—automatically assumed that I was of a higher social class, for instance. That would subsequently be translated in me getting special treatment everywhere that I went without anybody ever asking me any question because I was 'allowed'—*entitled even*—to be everywhere."

I smiled at his disclosure because I knew this was true, for I never understood why Vietnamese people were always treating foreigners (*and by foreigners, I mean white people*) in an overly nice manner. When growing up in Hanoi, I used to cringe whenever my foreigner friends and I would go to a coffee shop because I always noticed how the waiters would be excessively nice to my white friends compared to their behavior with customers at other tables.

Until this day, I still didn't have an answer to this question, other than my own presumption that it must be a sentiment of inferiority that had been sowed in the Vietnamese people, psychologically, throughout our war-filled history over the previous two centuries.

"Do you feel Vietnamese somehow, Tommy?" I asked him abruptly for no specific reason other than my curiosity. After living there for fifteen years—*more than I had*—he must have felt somewhat tied to the land and its people. And unsurprisingly, he confirmed his identity as an Asianized Westerner.

I laughed at that. *Of course he was. Look at his home decoration!*

He shared with me his deep respect for the discreet aspect of the Vietnamese culture. Most probably due to the fact that he lived in Vietnam his whole life before moving to France, Thomas had acquired a deep understanding of the importance of being humble from the Vietnamese culture. He knew Vietnamese people were never taught to showcase their strengths and it would actually be looked down upon if someone even mentioned their own accomplishments in a conversation—let alone bragged or boasted about them.

He confessed that these Vietnamese values—*discretion and humility*—he had acquired were quite problematic for him a couple of years back when he was going through job interviews to work for big corporations in France. He wished he wasn't so attached to these Vietnamese principles and ways of being. He wished he could have sold himself just a little bit better or simply talked a bit more about his accomplishments without feeling awkward about it.

But something within him prevented him from doing so and that something, according to Thomas, was definitely his Vietnamese flair.

"Are you happy in Paris now?" I asked him, genuinely curious about what he had to say.

Very matter-of-factly, he admitted to have romanticized Vietnam for many, many years.

"I don't think Vietnam was necessarily better; I was just more innocent and had better circumstances," he declared.

Although deep down I thought here was some truth to it, I wasn't ready to admit the "*Vietnam wasn't necessarily better*" part of his opinion. For me, Vietnam was still the best part of my life so far, in many different ways.

"That wasn't my question," I asserted in an offended manner.

"Yes, I am happy here," he said almost in a guilty voice, as if he had just betrayed me because of this admission. As if he had left me behind in the land of yesterdays. "Your happiness relies on your willingness to invest in where you are now," he proceeded with a lot of determination, the kind of determination of someone who had pondered this question for years already.

I loved the emphasis on the *now* in his sentence, on the present moment. I loved the way he framed happiness like a choice, a conscious decision, "an investment," as he called it.

One that you bet on constantly, day in, day out. And the result would look something like the person I was looking at today: a happy and content Thomas.

Truly in peace with his life choices.

The rest was superfluous.

NGỌC (BI) NGUYỄN: HOME IS ACCEPTANCE

Writing this book is, by far, one of the sweetest journeys of my life.

It makes me realize, for the first time, that I am no longer grieving the person I once thought I was or wanted to be. In retrospect, along with a lot of introspection, I figured the reason why I hated every single moment I spent in boarding school was simply because I was a child in grieving.

Boarding school happened to be the place where I went through four out of the five stages of the grieving process.

I first denied the fact that I was living there. I constantly had very interesting conversations with people in my head. I pretended I was still going to the clubs in Hanoi every chance I got. I ingested my friends' Facebook pictures and notifications like I would a huge tub of Ben and Jerry's cookie dough ice cream. And although my strong **Denial** kept me warmest during those cold Connecticut nights (like the extra six kilograms that I subsequently gained), Denial was also the biggest speed bump on my road to Acceptance.

Then came **Anger**, my worst enemy. *Oh how ugly it got sometimes.* I hated myself for always being so angry at everyone, but somehow it was always the easier alternative. My parents' *"hello darling"* sounded like mockery to my ears. My brother's Facebook updates were like the middle finger to my face. My friends' pictures were tolerated only because I always pretended I was still there with all of them.

And moments later I would hate them for forgetting me, the hatred so strong I sometimes didn't recognize myself.

At times, I wondered whether my friends had such intense thoughts about me. Whether they, too, hated me for abandoning them in the pursuit of what I thought was my American dream.

I tried **Bargaining** for some time but I knew from the very beginning it wasn't going to work. I bargained with Mom and Dad, begging them to let me come home and in exchange I would never go out again in my life, to no avail.

I told them I would be the most hardworking kid they had ever seen. No effect.

So I soldiered through and fell into a deep state of **Depression**—a place so hollow and lonely that until today, I still found it impossible to put words to it.

How can words—*anything for that matter*—describe a void?

I was so empty. I was emptied of every single thing that I had previously filled myself with: my city, my languages, my relationships.

And as I landed in America, I was also stripped of what I thought was intrinsically mine: my identity.

I was grieving so many things at the same time that I didn't know how to prioritize. What to grieve first? The death of my family life? The demise of an international community

I had always taken for granted? The loss of my childhood home, city, country?

Or, was it simply the death of the person I was before arriving in the United States? Was she the same person who sat with me on that trimestral fifteen-hour plane ride from Windsor back to Hanoi? Did I leave her behind upon boarding that first plane ride to the States? Was I meant to pick her up again only upon my visits?

And the biggest challenge of all: How was I going to persevere through invisibility in this new world where no one saw me as I saw myself?

And as if grieving my past was not enough, I also felt the need to grieve my future, simply because time was just so damn linear. All of the plans I made for the upcoming versions of myself—*all the people I was going to become!*—had completely collapsed in front of me. And so I was grieving the future that never happened as well.

So I depressed and depressed.

Fast forward a decade from my depression and I am now living in the state of **Acceptance**—the final and most enjoyable stage of the grieving process.

Final-fucking-ly.

Acceptance had come to stay for a while now. At the beginning, it came in bits and pieces, in short instances. I would catch a glimpse of it whenever I smiled at myself in the mirror. Other times it appeared in the lightness of the moment spent with friends, the genuineness of my feelings. And still other times it even walked with me to work, sat with me on trains, and boarded with me on planes.

And then slowly, seamlessly, acceptance came to stay for longer periods of time. It was a rather nice presence. I no longer constantly wished that I was somewhere else all the time. I no longer talked to people from my past, in my head. I no longer found myself intensely missing something—*a dish, a voice, a smell*—anymore.

At least not all the time.

And that was when I knew the life I dreamt of leading and the life I was actually living were one and the same.

Coincidentally—*is anything ever coincidental?*—as my grieving process came to an end, I found I had also accepted all of the different facets of my cultural identities. Instead of constantly asking myself dead-end questions, I let all of the cultures within me interact with one another freely, every day working out its own place within me.

I hear the different voices that each culture had inside my head. On more than one occasion, I listened to their conversations turned debates turned negotiations. I paid a lot of attention to the carefully crafted arguments each party brought out. Most of the time, I still found myself right in the middle of their argument: not fully rejecting one but also not fully accepting the other.

Until today, I still don't know whether it is better to wear shoes inside the house or take them off. *Is "better" even the right comparative to use?* So I do both. Some days I wear them, some days I don't.

But that's the easier debate.

Then you have the harder ones. Is fortune-telling a real science or a hoax? Should I have sweet or salty food for breakfast? Is Jesus more loving or Buddha?

And the list of debates goes on endlessly.

When reasons aren't enough to convince me—*they are never enough*—I shift my attention to the internal atmosphere these exchanges create in my chest. I follow the feelings that were surging at the moment and tell myself a piece of my identity resides within it. And that's the price to pay for having such a diverse cultural heritage.

As time passes, I have learned to sit with myself and to welcome all of the different cultural identities within me. I have even learned to make room within myself to welcome my American side—a cultural dimension of my identity I can no longer live without after almost a decade of residency in the States. Whenever I stroll down the streets in Paris, I find myself craving the American friendliness, and the American smile and easy conversation. I laugh at the minuscule plate sizes of most Parisian restaurants and regularly long for the heart-attack American cuisine.

I notice how I laugh—*instead of cry*—when I miss things that aren't in my reach.

Maybe I have been wrong all along.

Maybe I don't need proof of belonging to any of these cultures because I never really belonged to any one of them. I only belong to bits and pieces of them. Like an art collector, I pick out the best elements in each of the cultures I have encountered and display them proudly in the museum that is my life.

And going beyond the cultural dimension, I have learned there are many ways to answer the "Where are you from?" question. And it doesn't necessarily have to be a piece of land or a nation-state like I was once taught to believe.

I learned I can belong to people and cities and memories. I can belong to a shared habit, a favorite song, or a dance routine.

I belong to moments, both ones I remember and ones I don't (but are remembered by others).

Because ultimately, a person's cultural belonging has never been about where you've lived, but how you've lived.

And so it is.

ACKNOWLEDGMENTS

———

I would like to first thank my Mom, Dad, and Phatty. Thank you for your unwavering support even though none of you read any of my newsletters or social media posts. Your constant calls meant the world to me, especially when I was so far away throughout the entire pandemic season. Without your disturbances, I might have been able to finish this book six months earlier and stress-free. Thanks also for all the mental health issues you three have caused in my life; I wouldn't have half the number of stories I have today to share with the world otherwise.

(I really hope you read this thank you note.)

Thank you to my over one hundred interviewees. Even though I can't name each and every one of you here in this section, please know I am forever grateful to have spent time learning more about you. If while reading this book, you find pieces of yourself sprinkled in some chapters or hidden in some paragraphs, chances are I am writing about you! Thank you for opening up to me and for entrusting me with such a huge part of yourself.

Thank you to my beta readers without whom I will not be able to be half as happy as I am today with the final product:

- Thank you Aisha Babalakin for feeding me constant and brilliant feedback throughout my editing journey. Your opinion is one I have always highly valued, sincerely.
- Thank you Matthew Welch for always being supportive in everything I do (literally) despite the distance and time difference. I am lucky to count you among my friends.
- Thank you Thomas de Ruty for being so invested in the editing process of this book. I am so happy you granted me an interview and subsequently let me publish it!
- Thank you Sofia (Wifey) Galatas for constructively destroying my introduction (among other chapters) and for playing the role of the overly-critical reader; I desperately needed that (and you)!
- Thank you Claire and Steve for giving me such beautiful memories to write about and subsequently such in-depth comments from a completely different perspective to consider.
- Thank you the Llamas Tribe for our weekly calls and positive vibes and cooking lessons over Zoom and endless other things. I wouldn't have survived without you.

Thank you Nicolas Lemaire for caring for me when I didn't know how to care for myself.

Thank you Aimilia Theodoridis for being with me from day one of the IG journey for WCKs. I look forward to feeling lost and clueless in the years to come with you.

Thank you Diana Deeb Ishhab for tolerating me at my worst and loving me at my best.

Thank you Nguyễn Trâm Anh for the best logo I can ever ask for. And for the many hours of phone conversations, despite the distance and time difference.

Thank you Adam Phi Võ for maybe one day creating my official website.

Thank you to each and every one who took part in this journey with me whether through your time, support, conversation, understanding, creativity, or food donation. This book wouldn't exist without you all.

Thank you Professor Eric Koester of Georgetown University and Brian Bies of New Degree Press for this once-in-a-lifetime opportunity. I am so glad we found each other (in a non-romantic way, of course).

Last but not least, HUGE thank you to my editor Sarah Lobrot for all you did to help me put this book together. Thank you for being part of my dream-constructing journey and for believing in me and my sometimes weird vision of the book. I am immensely grateful to have met you and to have worked with you.

Dreams do come true.

Made in the USA
Middletown, DE
09 December 2020